God in history

The events of history form the framework which to a large extent determines the present. Christianity has been a key element in that framework. It claims a historical basis in the life, death and resurrection of Jesus Christ recorded in historical documents, the Gospels. How reliable are those documents? Did the events they recount actually happen, or are they of the order of Hindu and Buddhist myths and legends? In the first part of this book Dr Ives examines the evidence from a historian's perspective, and discusses the Christian claim that God has acted in human affairs.

In the second part he takes a series of case-studies on the place of Christianity in history. Whose side was God on in the Reformation? Did capitalism rise out of Christian ethics, or was it an economic movement that coincided with the rise of Christian entrepreneurs? Who spun the intricate web of church-state relations in the sixteenth century? How far was the church compromised when kings marched to war with Christ on their banners?

Dr Ives is Senior Lecturer in Modern History at Birmingham University.

An Aslan Lion Book

GOD IN HISTORY

E. W. Ives

LION PUBLISHING

Contents

Preface

Authors regularly claim in a preface that the credit for anything of value in their work belongs to others, but that the errors are their own. In the case of this book the claim is no mere convention. These chapters are the product of discussion and debate with numerous friends, professional colleagues and students in the course of historical study, teaching and communication and also in the fellowship of the Christian church.

In particular I would mention those who read the manuscript at various stages – John Briggs, John Day, Robert Knecht, Alison Marsh, Philip McNair and Derek Wood – and Ruth Ives, my most long-suffering critic. If these find the book now more accurate, more lucid and more compelling they have only themselves to thank.

Notes have been kept to a minimum, but I have attempted to give references to all quotations. These are grouped at the end of each chapter; where several references are found in a single paragraph, these are consolidated under one note number. Biblical references are to *The New English Bible* (1970) throughout.

E.W. Ives
Warwick, February 1977

Introduction

'Three fundamental questions puzzle the modern believer and turn away the would-be convert to Christianity.'[1] Is there really a spiritual world? What do the statements of the ancient creeds and confessions of the church mean in today's language? How can Christians continue to hold that the life of Jesus Christ has unique, eternal reference when we know that the world and the human race are infinitely older than we once supposed?

With these questions Lord Hailsham, the former Lord Chancellor has drawn attention to the need to rethink the Christian faith in twentieth-century terms. This book is concerned with a limited aspect of the second question. In what sense can Christianity still be regarded as a historical religion, a religion which claims to be rooted in actual events in history and also claims to be fulfilled in history?

The object is not a study in divinity; I am no theologian. Nor, in the normal sense, is it an essay in apologetics. The approach is down-to-earth and arises from my personal position as a professional historian who is also, by conviction, a Christian and so in honesty bound to grapple with the relation between the two. Of course my standpoint is that of commitment, and commitment grounded in Protestant non-conformity. But it is the commitment which gives urgency to the task. The stark choice is between a Christianity which buries its head in the sand and refuses to ask questions and a faith which is prepared to face the reality of the past.

Discussion is here divided into two parts. The first looks at the issues which are raised because Christianity claims to have originated in historical events and to offer a distinctive interpretation of the way history works. The second section turns from the general to the particular and explores the relationship between Christianity and history at certain key periods and in certain crucial episodes in the past. These are taken largely from the sixteenth and seventeenth centuries and are discussed both for their intrinsic importance and as exemplars of the need for Christian comment on history.

The problems selected have arisen in the course of my own teaching and research and many others deserve equal consideration. But my objective is not to provide an encyclopedia of answers so much as to share approaches to problems in the Christian philosophy of history and to those problems as seen in actual historical episodes. And if this book suggests questions to ask, avenues to explore and attitudes to criticize, it will have served its purpose.

Note
1   *The Times*, 21 February 1976.

Part 1

HISTORY AND
THE CHRISTIAN FAITH

Chapter 1

Where Christianity and history meet

Conflict between science and religion has been with us for many years, and acutely so for the last century. It has attracted many notable contenders on each side and given rise to a vast literature on the subject, both popular and learned. By contrast, the relationship between history and Christianity has been little noticed in the Anglo-Saxon world, and literature on the topic is neither plentiful nor palatable. That Herbert Butterfield's *Christianity and History*, published in 1949, is a conspicuous exception on both counts only accentuates the point.

For many people there is no problem; history has no conflict with religion. It has nothing to say about the existence or non-existence of God, about ethics or about life after death. Yet there is a problem. Christianity specifically asserts its truth in terms of historical events, above all the career and personality of a first-century Middle-eastern Jew, Jesus Christ. The creeds of the church make this absolutely clear. They force home the historical basis for the faith: 'Jesus Christ...suffered under Pontius Pilate, was crucified, dead and buried.' Christianity proclaims that it is founded on historical fact and the assertion cannot be evaded.

Christianity, of course, claims to be more than mere history; it holds up Jesus Christ as a phenomenon of cosmic and eternal significance. Equally it asks for much more than an intellectual response; it demands personal commitment. But everything rests on the assumption that what is said to have happened in Palestine in the first century AD did happen. Not all Christian thinkers and scholars would go along with this. Some would argue that whatever significance Christ has must be quarried from a sediment of myth and tradition, that the search for a historical Jesus must end in frustration. Others would assert that historical fact or lack of fact is irrelevant; what matters is current religious experience. But it is hard to see how anything specifically 'Christian' can survive without a 'historical Christ', or how an existential faith can be defended if it rests on nothing at all. If Christianity is not rooted in actual history then it is a giant delusion.

The first relationship of history to Christianity is, therefore, that the factual claims of Christianity need to be tested. A further dimension arises from what Christianity teaches about human history. In common with orthodox Judaism, Christianity maintains that events move under the authority of God according to an ultimate purpose and, moreover, that they exhibit the operation in history of a moral judgement. God is the God of history and the judge of the earth. For the Christian this is seen in terms of the present lordship and final triumph of Jesus Christ. Again the creeds are insistent. '[He] sits on the right hand of God the Father' – the position of rule and authority; 'he shall come again in glory to judge both the living and the dead.'

In practice, both the concept of purpose and the notion of judgement in history are open to much abuse. All too often believers apply them in the crudest fashion imaginable. Convinced that history will demonstrate these truths, they inevitably find what they are looking for; faith, not historical judgement is at work, and for the student of history that is not good enough. Since Christianity teaches that God is working in the world, the historian is bound to ask: How? and Where? and How do you know? Similarly, if morality is built into the universe, ought there not to be some sign of it? It is all too easy for the individual to sing in church 'God is working his purpose out' and never to ask what that means.

To relate history and Christianity in this way is to raise yet another problem. Scholarship today divides understanding of a phenomenon among a number of self-contained disciplines. Each offers within its own terms a complete statement and each has its own rules and attitudes. Each is autonomous; criteria proper to one are not proper to another. 'God' is not a satisfactory answer to the 'why' of the historian. Yet the Christian historian believes in a God who works in human affairs. Just as 'sets' in modern mathematics overlap giving an area common to both, so the apparently separate history and religion overlap; history is only partial with God left out and religion divorced from history is mutilated. If this is so, can the Christian honestly omit from an essay or discussion such a vital element simply in deference to current assumptions about the way knowledge is organized? Is it not as justifiable to claim that Luther was driven by the Spirit of God as by nationalism, psychological compulsion or even constipation?

History relates to Christianity also at one of the most sensitive points of religion, the assertion that Christianity is unique, distinct from the other great religions of the world in kind, rather than in details of doctrine. The ground for such a claim is an historical one. Christianity offers no wisdom; it is not a religion of those who seek enlightenment. It has nothing to say of self-help; it does not promise man a programme to attain to salvation. It does not provide, unless by analogy, a ritual or myth to express the great realities of life and death, light and darkness. Instead it alleges that particular events in history were a final and supreme revelation of God, by God. The historian is not equipped to go into dogma and comparative religion but this alleged distinctiveness in Christian revelation is within his competence. Neither Buddhist nor Muslim teaching rejects Jesus Christ; the Hindu accepts that there are 'many ways to God'. Is the exclusiveness of Christianity well founded or an arrogant refusal to listen to others?

These, then, are some of the meeting points of Christianity and history and the theme of the first part of this book.

Chapter 2

A question of evidence

The Bible is a leather-bound book with gold edges and the adjective 'Holy' embossed on the cover – or so many people would say. Christians give it a special veneration and accept its authority. Communities in many parts of the world use it on solemn occasions of public and private life and still expect the truth to be sworn in court with the holy book in the right hand. Other religions too have their sacred writings – the Torah, the Koran, the Dhammapada, the Vedas – which are likewise given special reverence and care. 'Holy writings' seem to be in a category different to other books, to be approached in a duly humble and believing manner. But not by the historian.

Whatever their supernatural or spiritual claims, sacred scriptures are books which arose in particular historical contexts. They are just as amenable to technical investigation as any other literature. They command no special exemption and can claim no automatic authority. As Gershwin's song puts it,

> The things that you're li'ble
> To read in the Bible,
> It ain't necessarily so.

The importance of this historical scrutiny will be greater or less according to the religion in question. Where the historical component is slight, as in Hinduism, the historian will have little to say. With Christianity and its root in an alleged historical episode, what he has to say will be of crucial significance. A faith which claims to rest upon actual events must stand or fall by the evidence which establishes those events. To know what the truth is must, after all, be more important than having faith; there can be no possible merit in a religion founded on fiction.

For early Christianity and its founder, the historical evidence is of two kinds: a little in pagan and Jewish writings and a much larger amount from Christian sources. At once this looks suspicious. Is the evidence about Jesus Christ any more than the propaganda of pious believers? It would, in fact, be no surprise if the story of Jesus were entirely unknown in non-Christian sources; the proper measure of comparison is the thousands of other Jews crucified by the Roman Empire of whom we know nothing at all. It would have been most improbable for one particular Jewish artisan who fell foul of the provincial government of first-century Palestine to attract special attention at the time or for any formal record to have survived. But some time later significant material does begin to appear in non-Christian (and usually hostile) sources, just at the point where what had begun as the private faith of a few of Christ's followers was becoming a matter for public notice.

The opposition evidence

The most reliable evidence (reliable because found in official correspondence rather than in literary narrative) occurs at the turn of the first century in the letters of Pliny the Younger, the imperial legate in Bithynia (Western Turkey), to the Emperor Trajan (98–117), asking advice on the treatment of Christians. At much the same time Tacitus was writing, and in his *Annals* tells of the Emperor Nero blaming the fire of Rome of AD 64 upon the Christians and initiating a savage persecution of the sect. Their name, he explains, was derived from one 'Christus' who was executed by the procurator (governor) of Judea, Pontius Pilate, in the reign of the Emperor Tiberius (14–37). Suetonius, again writing at the start of the second century, includes in his *Lives of the Caesars* a reference to Nero's persecution. He may also be reporting previous unrest at Rome over Christianity when he records the expulsion of the Jews from the city in about AD 49 as a result of trouble caused by 'a certain Chrestus'. This seems the more likely because the story of Christ's death was known in Rome by about AD 50 when the historian Thallus attempted to give a naturalistic explanation of certain of the events of Good Friday.

Taken together these sources reveal a good deal about early Christianity. Pontius Pilate was procurator of Judea between AD 26 and 37. 'Christus' was not a surname but the Greek translation of 'Messiah', the title Jews gave to the God-given deliverer their religion promised. Pliny also makes it clear that his enquiries indicated that in his day Christus was regarded by his followers as a god. At the start of the second century, therefore, Roman public men (as all of them were) are agreed that the founder of this troublesome religion was a Palestinian executed some seventy years earlier, initially identified with the national expectations of the Jewish people, but now seen as divine.

With the principal Jewish source, the writings of the turncoat Flavius Josephus, the situation is more complicated. He was born in the year AD 37/38 and was active in Jewish politics in the two decades before the revolt against Rome which ended with the destruction of Jerusalem in AD 70. Thereafter he became an imperial pensioner at Rome, spending his time writing history. Thus Josephus was in a position to know a great deal about the origin of Christianity. He records the career of John the Baptist and certainly knew of the existence of Jesus because in his *Antiquities of the Jews* (written about AD 90) he refers to the death of James 'the brother of Jesus, the so-called Christ'.[1] In another passage he tells of the crucifixion of Christ by Pilate but the text has been tampered with by the insertion of a reference to the resurrection, presumably the work of a Christian apologist.

Since Josephus was writing to argue Jewish (and his own) respectability, it is not surprising that he says nothing more about the unfortunate bastard, Christianity. But this is enough to confirm what the Roman writers say, that Jesus existed and was crucified by the Roman governor Pontius Pilate in Palestine before AD 37, that his followers survived and were known as Christians.

What is also important about this pagan and Jewish testimony is its date. We have firm, hostile evidence of Christianity from not more than seventy or eighty years after Christ's execution. And if Tacitus is correct in what he says of Nero, (and he was a young boy at the time), a distinctive group of Christ's followers were well established in Rome earlier than that, within thirty years of his death. The historical existence of Jesus Christ, the Jewish founder of Christianity, his execution by Rome, his alleged Messiahship and deification by his followers are beyond question.

The earliest friendly sources

For detailed information about Christ we are, on the other hand, wholly dependent on Christian sources. These are of three kinds. The earliest are letters to a number of Christian congregations, 'the Epistles'; next are formal narratives of the life of Christ and the early church, 'the Gospels' and the so-called 'Acts of the Apostles'; thirdly there are the writings of second-generation Christians and later, 'the Fathers'.

The order: Epistles – Gospels may seem backwards to readers familiar with the New Testament, but it is important to recognize that the earliest sources for Christianity are the Epistles, with their evidence of active communities of believers, not the narratives about Christ. Not every scholar would put a first-century date on every letter in the New Testament canon, nor accept all the traditions of authorship, but the basic letters of Paul can be safely placed in the decade or so following AD 50 when, perhaps, the earliest was written. And given a bare minimum of Paul's letters, those to the churches in Thessaloniki, Galatia, Corinth and Rome, we have enough to construct the fundamental tenets of Christianity. Without question the story of a crucified but resurrected saviour named Jesus who was identified with the Jewish Messiah and already described as the Son of God was known hundreds of miles from its Palestinian starting point within twenty years of the crucifixion.

Paul's letters, indeed, give us glimpses of even earlier than this. From time to time these include material either where he refers to a standard syllabus of Christian preaching, the *kerygma*, or where he repeats an evident hymn or saying which he expects his readers to know. The faith which we find in the letters was already well formulated. Perhaps most striking are the Aramaic words he occasionally uses which were clearly familiar to European Christians but can only be persistent elements of a tradition going back to the original Palestinian churches – the intimate addressing of God as *Abba,* Father, or the prayer *Marana tha,* 'Our Lord come!', which clearly shows that the earliest Jewish believers prayed to Christ as Lord.[2]

Dating the Gospels

The Gospels, by contrast, belong not to the initial period of Christian expansion but to the first stages of consolidation, to days when the generation of eyewitnesses who had seen Jesus or the apostles at first hand was dying out. Matthew, Mark and Luke share much common material, and in consequence are called the Synoptic (parallel) Gospels; John is probably later since it organizes the story in a conscious and stylized manner. Wild estimates of the possible date of the Gospels have been made in the past and are still heard, but papyrus discoveries in this century include a compilation not later than AD 150 which shows knowledge of all four texts, and a fragment of John, discovered in Egypt and datable to about AD 130. The latter would suggest a latest composition date for the fourth Gospel of about AD 100, and thus an earlier date for the Synoptics.[3]

More approximate dating for the first three Gospels depends upon their relationship, and this is a vexed problem. Matthew includes over 90 per cent of Mark in various ways, and Luke somewhat less, but 5 per cent of Mark is found in neither of the other two. Matthew and Luke each have exclusive matter as well, and also share material in common but not with Mark. The problem is complicated by the possibility that some verbal differences may have been eliminated as the Gospels began to circulate together, or idiosyncrasies produced by accidents of transmission, or both. Nevertheless the consensus is that Matthew and Luke borrow from Mark, rather than the reverse, and also that they probably share a lost common source or sources (by convention labelled 'Q'); in addition they had sources of their own. If, then we can date Mark, we have some 'earliest possible date' for the other two. Most scholars would assign Mark to the sixties of the first century, in part because it appears to antedate the destruction of Jerusalem in AD 70. Matthew, then, might be twenty years or so later, say AD 85–90.

With Luke there is an additional factor – its companion volume, the Acts of the Apostles; the dating of one is clearly affected by the dating of the other. Acts takes the story of the early church to AD 60/61 but does not deal with the Neronian persecution of AD 64 nor with the fate of the book's principal figure, Paul of Tarsus. This would argue for a date in the early sixties for Acts and the point is made stronger if the aims of the book are examined. These were to convince pagan readers of the respectability of Christianity and to edify believers both by the story of apostolic times and by the Christian teaching it enshrines. But how could the book succeed with either if it ignored the first assault by the state on the church? Christians had been denounced for 'abominations'. Were these not to be rebutted? Christians, probably Paul himself, had died as martyrs. Was their example to go unnoticed? A date before AD 64 seems strongly indicated. Yet Acts is the second part of a pair with Luke and, as we have seen, Luke must post-date Mark.

The problems are clear. One way out is the suggestion that Luke as we now have it was built up in two stages, a version without the material from Mark which was followed by Acts and later expanded into the present text, say in the early eighties. The hypothesis is attractive, but it is only a hypothesis. For the layman who wishes to avoid the bewilderment of textual theories the simple conclusion seems to be a date for the final version of Luke of five years either side of AD 80.

Of more interest than the possibility of texts which evolved over a period of time is the suggestion that there were probably sources behind the present gospels. 'Q' may have been a collection or collections of the sayings of Christ in a framework akin to one of the Old Testament prophetic books. Its language was Greek, but clear evidence of Aramaic elements shows that it derived from a Palestinian original, perhaps oral, perhaps written. Those who argue that this presumed antecedent of 'Q' was written, find support in a comment by Papias, a bishop early in the second century in what is now Western Turkey. He made a deliberate effort to collect early Christian memories and reports that: 'Matthew compiled the Logia [oracles or sayings] in Hebrew [Aramaic] speech, and everyone translated them as best he could'.[4] But even if we reject this and assume that the material of 'Q' was not committed to writing until in Greek translation, we still have the important conclusion that the Gospels reached their present form based, in part at least, on earlier written material which had its origin in the nursery of the Christian faith, in Jerusalem and Galilee.

One point about the New Testament texts which must impress the historian is that they are very extensive compared with other writings of the period. All we know of Tacitus' *Annals* and *Histories* is what is preserved in two manuscripts; his minor works survive in a single copy. Many of the most famous classical authors also are known only through late texts; the earliest Tacitus dates from the ninth century AD, and so too does Caesar's *Gallic War*, while the same is true (apart from scraps) of the older Greek historians, Thucydides and Herodotus. Furthermore, many events and individuals are known to us through single sources only; nowhere is there any density of coverage, multiple accounts of a single individual and his impact.

By contrast, New Testament manuscripts are plentiful, early and varied. Nor is it merely a matter of manuscripts; there is the witness of the church as embodied in the writings of the early Fathers. Many of these belong to the later second and subsequent centuries and are not authoritative for the earlier periods, but the Apostolic Fathers, those church leaders writing in the period AD 90 to 150, are of importance. Their references and quotations help to establish both the texts of particular works and also the canon or list of the sacred books which circulated among the early churches. They also preserve the traditions and memories of the Christians who lived between fifty and a hundred years after the death of Christ. Papias not only suggests a possible origin for 'Q', but records that the Gospel of Mark represents the message preached by the apostle Peter which was preserved in writing by his 'interpreter' Mark. A letter from about AD 96 attributed to Clement of Rome tells of the fate of Peter and Paul, martyred in the city some thirty years earlier. Ignatius of Smyrna also refers to their deaths at Rome in a letter of about the year 110. The conclusion seems inescapable: there is overwhelming evidence that the New Testament documents are authentic sources for the life of Jesus Christ and the faith of his immediate disciples.

Rose-tinted glasses?

Authenticity, however, is not the same as reliability. Can we be sure that pious enthusiasm is not responsible for the signs and wonders recorded in the New Testament and intentional propaganda for the force of the story? The problem of the miraculous is the theme of the next chapter. As for the evident bias of Christian writings, this is frankly declared by the documents themselves. They are not coolly impartial accounts. They set out the faith which the church was dedicated to promote; their purpose is to bring men to believe. This is not to say that they are works of fiction, constructed only for effect. The factual nature of Christian claims put a premium on accuracy, as Luke, at least, openly admitted. He began his Gospel with these words:

> Many writers have undertaken to draw up an account of the events that have happened among us, following the traditions handed down to us by the original eyewitnesses and servants of the gospel. And so I in my turn...as one who has gone over the whole course of these events in detail, have decided to write a connected narrative for you, so as to give you authentic knowledge about the matters of which you have been informed.[5]

It would have been folly to risk discredit for carelessness and worse.

Commitment, however, is another matter, and the New Testament writers are committed. This is what explains the contrasts between the Gospels. Their object is not a biography of Christ but the presentation of a religious statement about him which is very much that of the particular author. The Gospel of Mark may even be arranged around the instruction given to converts. It appears to be a digest of the facts of the gospel, arranged in an order for believers to remember, an amplified version of the stylized preaching found elsewhere in the New Testament. Mark does not set out all he knows about Christ; he puts down what converts needed to know in the most economical way for them to remember.

Before the Gospels

The role of commitment in shaping the Christian story is even more obvious if the question is asked, 'How did the message circulate before being reduced to writing?' The temptation is to assume that this stage of oral transmission was unorganized and unselective, with the Gospel writers choosing and arranging subsequently, as a modern biographer would. Oral traditions, however, do not seem to work like that. Memorized material tends to circulate in various patterns or 'forms' and is influenced by the purpose for which the material is remembered. The most familiar modern analogy is a statement made to the police by a witness. The witness tells the story as fully as he can, often emphasizing the part he played, but the policeman will put the words into a set order and pattern, omitting extraneous matter and highlighting points of significance. The evidence is then in the 'form' required by the law.

One immediate consequence of applying this suggestion to the oral stage of the Christian gospel is to increase historical confidence in the reliability of the eventual text; the message had previously circulated in definite forms, not as random gossip. But to identify that message, the process known as form-criticism must try to go further, to isolate the particular oral pattern behind the text and determine the life-situation which produced and preserved it. In the case of the police witness, the pattern is the formal statement and the life-situation the interview with a policeman and the subsequent court case. What then of the oral Christian gospel?

Clearly we are in a highly conjectural area; we cannot get much further than 'perhaps', 'possibly' and (rarely) 'probably'. But form critics would agree that there are several different patterns for the oral gospel material, such as a passion narrative (an account of Christ's last days and of his execution), stories which focus on some pronouncement by Jesus, miracle stories which emphasize him as a worker of wonders, parables and sayings and, lastly, a handful of particular incidents in his life, such as his baptism in the River Jordan. Without question, this material was preserved by the early church community and the forms into which it was organized reflect the conviction of the community that Jesus was the God-given Saviour.

Initially, of course, there would have been a multiplicity of individual memories of Christ's life and sayings, but under the pressures of preaching and teaching this unselective stage could not last. The religiously significant material would soon be sifted from purely personal reminiscence and take on forms reflecting that significance – just as in the case of the police-witness. Something of the sort would clearly explain the account of Christ's passion which from the earliest stage seems to have been a connected narrative, a contrast with the rest of the Gospel material which is evident even today in translation. There was no great religious significance in a detailed account of the rest of Christ's life, but there was for his last few days and so it was preserved. Christian commitment, therefore, is integral to the very content and shape of the gospel story.

Yet commitment, of itself, is no necessary bar to accuracy and certainly no novelty to the historian. How to assess a text originally written from a partisan standpoint, how to distinguish what a writer wanted to be believed, indeed believed himself, from what the truth was, such problems are commonplace in historical scholarship. Christianity would only be a special case if the Gospel material organized by the primitive church did not substantially derive from Christ. If that were to be the case we should have no reliable source and could know nothing of the historical Jesus, merely what his followers claimed about him.

A number of form critics have alleged that this is precisely the case. They argue that the early Christian community was not simply the life-situation in which the gospel tradition was organized, but the life-situation in which it was formed. What we now have reflects, therefore, the context and concerns of the early church, its evangelism, its controversies with Jewish communities, the growth of its worship and so forth. The church was not so much referring back to an authoritative founder as interpreting its founder in the light of its later experiences; gospel incidents could even be subsequent events projected back into the life of Jesus.

A historian may be forgiven for thinking this scepticism is exaggerated and unconvincing. There was no lengthy period for legend to emerge; Paul's letters show that traditions were already fixed at an early stage. In any case the gospel circulated in an exclusively oral form for only thirty years, that is up to the appearance of Mark, and less than that if 'Q' antedates the first Gospel. What is more, the home of the oral tradition was Palestine, so that any development could only have taken place against widely disseminated individual recollections of Christ; what the church taught its converts could not have conflicted with what was common knowledge. Even more striking, the urgent problems of the early church are scarcely touched upon in the Synoptic Gospels or in what we know of 'Q', most notably the question of whether or not to circumcise Gentile converts.

A far more credible life-situation for the oral gospel is the remarkable impact which Jesus Christ had upon his disciples. Certainly the teaching about Christ was formalized within the early Christian community, but it originated with Christ, just as the form of the police statement does not alter what the witness saw. The effect which Jesus had on his followers was powerful enough, whatever one makes of the facts, to convince them that he was alive again after being crucified; that they should also have had a sharp recollection of his life and words is no surprise at all. It may even be that some Christian forms derived from Christ's own teaching. Despite their dependence upon translation, English readers can still see the way in which his sayings exhibit rhythm and conscious parallelism. Analysis of the Greek text suggests that in the Aramaic original much of his teaching was cast in a poetic and prophet-like style, easy to remember. Some scholars have gone further and argued that Christ supervised the memorizing of his words by his disciples in the same way that Jewish rabbis did. Despite the evident partisan nature and proselytizing purpose of the Christian gospel, there is no reason to believe that the oral stage of its transmission failed to preserve the facts of the historical Christ.

The purpose of this chapter has been to take a common-sense historical look at the evidence for New Testament Christianity. And viewed from that standpoint the evidence seems to be satisfactory. The essential Christian claims are set out in pagan and Jewish sources seventy or eighty years after the death of Christ and in the earliest Christian evidence, the Epistles, twenty years after that event. Although the Gospels are later than the Epistles, they are not discredited; all fall between AD 60 and 100, with good reason to place some material at the earlier date, that is thirty or thirty-five years after the crucifixion. What scholarship has discovered of the build-up of the text encourages confidence also. Bias there certainly is, most noticeably in the alleging of miracles and divine favour. Nevertheless, as C.H.Dodd wrote,

> I believe that a sober and instructed criticism of the Gospels justifies the belief that in their central and dominant tradition they represent the testimony of those who stood nearest to the facts, and whose life and outlook had been moulded by them.[6]

Notes and references

1 Josephus, *Works*, ed. W.Whiston, Ward Lock, 1878, p. 502.
2 Romans 8:15; 1 Corinthians 16:22; Galatians 4:6.
3 J.A.T.Robinson, *Redating the New Testament*, Mowbrays, 1976, pp.307,352, has strongly argued for the dating of the first version of John to AD 50/55 and the bulk of the New Testament to the period AD 50–70.
4 F.F.Bruce, *The New Testament Documents*, IVP, 5th edition 1960, p. 38.
5 Luke 1:1–4.
6 C.H.Dodd, *The Apostolic Preaching and its Developments*, Hodder and Stoughton, 1963, p. 56.

Chapter 3

Approaching the miraculous

The New Testament documents can be confidently attributed to the generation of the events they describe, but many modern scholars have been reluctant to accept this. The reason is not blindness to the evidence but disquiet at the consequences which seem to follow from accepting an early date. Archibald Robertson put this well when arguing against an early date for the Acts of the Apostles:

> The nature of the narrative of the Acts, starting from the physical ascension of Christ into heaven, and punctuated by miraculous gifts of tongues, cures, killings and escapes from prison, surely discounts it as history and stamps it as romance. An exception may be made in favour of journey-narratives written in the first person, which it is difficult to believe were invented. But further than this we can hardly go.[1]

The revealing phrase is: 'it is difficult to believe were invented'. The reasoning is: miracles belong to romance, hence they must be interpolations or additions to any core of original material, therefore of late date.

In fact, if miraculous elements are dismissed as incredible it does not necessarily follow that Christian evidence must be late in date. Certainly history does have many examples of individuals whose stories acquire legendary accretions over the years. Many people accept that William Shakespeare left Stratford after a poaching episode; the tale first appears more than a century after the alleged event, it is intrinsically improbable and there is no evidence to support it. Yet although the more likely explanation of many fables in history may be that they are later accretions, this is not always the case. First-hand narrators are not necessarily immune from misunderstanding, hallucination or sheer fantasy, especially when reporting under the influence of a powerful personality. In the case of the New Testament, how we date the documents and what we make of the miracles they record, are quite separate questions.

The 'historic' Christ

If the problem of the miraculous cannot be removed by redating the Gospels, it is obvious to ask instead, whether we can strip away the non-natural in the hope of discovering the 'historic' Christ. All attempts to do so have failed. A supernatural element is integral to the evidence in the earliest forms we can recover.

There is, for example, no more persistent Christian tradition than the association of the phrase 'three days' or 'the third day' with the death and resurrection of Christ. Not only is it hard to imagine any such phrase being added during the building up of a tradition, but its occurrence in several different traditions shows that it can only be an original element in the story. Paul mentions 'the third day' as part of the *kerygma* in a letter to Greek Christians some twenty years after the alleged event; it is found on five occasions in Mark and so passed into synoptic material; it is preserved in the non-synoptic verses of Luke and possibly also in the material exclusive to Matthew; it is found, once again independently, in a passage of probable Aramaic origin in Acts. Jesus was not a teacher who was gradually credited with divine qualities by successive generations of followers; the qualities are part of the primitive story.

Oliver Cromwell asked to be painted 'warts and all' and the historian has to accept that the Christian sources contain unavoidable material which will strain his credulity. He may decide that he cannot accept this material as true, but there is no warrant for making Christianity less offensive by cutting out the awkward pieces. It may be uncomfortable to consider that Christians were from the outset gullible, unbalanced, over-enthusiastic, mistaken or even correct, but these are the possibilities we have to face.

Are miracles impossible?

If we cannot dissect out the supernatural from the Christian story, that for many is the end. Miracles simply do not occur, and we cannot be expected to take seriously a narrative which says that they do. Put this way the case is attractive. Miracles do invite scepticism, for example the wonders attributed to a miscellany of medieval holy men. Yet the issue is not the improbability of miracles – nobody doubts that. It is their impossibility, the conclusion that it is more probable that men should lie, be mistaken, be deluded than that an event should ever contradict our experience. Anything is more probable than a miracle.

The weakness of such a view is that despite appearances it is not a reasoned conclusion, it is an assertion and no more. It masquerades as logic in David Hume's vigorous *Essay on Miracles* (1748):

> There must be a uniform experience against every miraculous event, otherwise the event would not merit that appellation. And as an uniform experience amounts to a proof, there is here a direct and full proof from the nature of the fact, against the evidence of miracle.[2]

But this rests on the assertion that nature is uniform, which is precisely what is in dispute. Hume says the uniformity is absolute, the believer in miracles says that it is not, and the matter rests in an exchange of dogmas. It is, as Hume knew, quite impossible to prove uniformity. Any argument against miracle constructed on the basis of probability must be a circular one; probability itself is only an assumption based upon the belief that nature is uniform. Odds in horse racing depend on the probabilities assessed by punters or assumptions about the previous experience and performance of horses, and yet outsiders continue to win. And although the probabilities of being killed when falling from an aeroplane without a parachute are infinitely greater, logically they are of the same kind, and individuals have survived.

Much of the respect for Hume's arguments can be explained by the scientific attitudes of the eighteenth-century world. Belief in a mechanistic universe operating according to fixed laws made a miracle appear as senseless as a screwdriver thrust into the works of a highly intricate watch. Scientists in the twentieth century have, however, ceased to think in such terms. They are much more aware of the limitation which scientific statements have and now admit 'randomness' as an inescapable factor in nature. Christians, too, have stopped asserting that they possess the only total explanation of all phenomena. They now admit that they offer only one way among many of describing events. For a Christian to say 'God created man' and a scientist to say: 'man evolved' is not necessarily incompatible.

On the issue of miracle Christianity has met science half way. It now realizes that the Bible does not treat miracle as an assault upon nature but instead sees miracle and nature as equally the activity of a God whose existence is a precondition for all existence. God acts, and if this action is repetitive and predictable we call it nature; if surprising or not within our current knowledge we call it miracle. The consequence is that there is no sense in which a miracle is unscientific.

Miracles – a question of proof

But the problem of miracle to the historian is neither a matter of logic nor of science, but a matter of proof. If unexpected events may happen, what can the historian know of them? Sometimes, of course, he will find no problem since the unexpectedness was in the mind of observers, not in the nature of the event. Many alleged miracles are of this sort; the aptness of the episode is what counts, not its improbability. The River Jordan has dried up opposite Jericho on a number of recorded occasions as a consequence of landslides upstream; the miracle for the Jews under Joshua was that this happened at precisely the time they wished to cross. The evacuation at Dunkirk in 1940 is often described as a miracle, yet it was possible because, among other things, mistakes were made by the German High Command. There is nothing unusual in military errors; it was the coincidence which caused people to think of miracle.

There are, however, events which are allegedly unexpected *per se* and do not fall into the category of 'appropriateness miracles'. The resurrection of Christ is the obvious example. Can the historian admit miracle in these cases? The answer would seem to be 'no'. Historical explanation is, in the first place, possible only within the terms of normal human experience; this alone give us a standard by which to judge. A resurrection would be a 'one-off' event and there are no criteria by which to judge the unique.

In 1976 the Roman Catholic Church decided that a Glasgow cancer patient had recovered miraculously as a result of prayer through a particular martyr. Whether or not a miracle did occur the historian cannot say; he is in no position to do so. He can admit the unexpected and even the inexplicable, but not more than this. He has no means of establishing whether anything outside normal experience has been involved. It is this which keeps a certain brand of popular pseudo-science writing in business; the crew of the Marie Celeste may have been seized by a spacecraft manned by little green men from Mars, but how are we to know? And it is really quite dishonest to assert that since the historian cannot 'prove' what happened, then the miracle is established, whether it be the resurrection of Jesus or the capture of a ship's crew.

What the historian can say

This conclusion may seem to be a confession of defeat. The historian admits that the unexpected is neither logically nor scientifically impossible, yet because it is unexpected he cannot identify it. But that would be to misunderstand the character of the statements the historian is entitled to make. A great deal of confusion is caused in history by loose usage of terms such as 'proof' and 'fact', which can and do mean very different things in different contexts. Take an illustration from 1815. It is a 'fact' that a battle was fought outside Brussels on Sunday 18 June, involving French, Prussian, British and other troops. It is also a 'fact' that the famous charge of the Scots Greys and other British heavy cavalry ended in a disaster which, for the rest of the battle, gave the French a highly dangerous superiority in mounted troops. It is a 'fact', yet again, that 'Wellington won the Battle of Waterloo', and every schoolboy knows it.

Here are three 'facts', but the meaning of the word is different in each case. 'There was a battle...' means that the sources agree that a conflict took place. 'A key factor was...' means that analysis of the sources seems to indicate that this or that episode had a particular importance. 'The battle was won by...' means that the historian has assessed the whole story and come to a judgement. These are three quite distinct orders of statement, corresponding to the questions 'What happened?' 'How did it happen?' and 'What meaning should we draw from it?'

Defined strictly, only one type of historical material has claim to objective reality, that is to exist quite independent of the observer. This is the data we discover in the original sources. Whatever we make of it, however we disagree about its significance, it is there, very much as readings and measurements taken at a scientific experiment are 'there'. Collecting data is the first stage of the historical process. The second is assessing it. This is a matter of assigning relative weight to individual items and exploring possible relationships and disconnections, probing – because this is history and not natural science – motives as well as action. Proposing a general conclusion or hypothesis is the final stage, a considered verdict by the historian. In a single enquiry he has moved from detective to counsel and has ended up as a jury of one. Thus we can say that the fact 'Wellington, won the Battle of Waterloo' is a hypothesis and no more. Even the name enshrines the supposition that it was a British victory – it was the Duke's rear headquarters which was at Waterloo, the actual battlefield was more than three miles away.

Given that history follows this methodology, the historian who declines to pronounce on miracle is not dodging the issue. He is taking a deliberately professional position. He does not say that miracles do not occur, simply that he cannot start to offer a hypothesis because a hypothesis which one way or the other involves the supernatural is outside his terms of reference.

However, this is not the same as saying that the historian has nothing at all to tell us about miracles. Before the stage of hypothesis must come the collection and assessment of data and these take place irrespective of any allegedly miraculous element. This is the historian's home territory; faced with the unexplained he has the duty to assemble the evidence and scrutinize what he finds. While he will not be able to say positively what any oddity was, he is in a position to exclude as many possibilities as he can. His job, in other words, is to establish that something odd has or has not occurred.

At this point a critic might object that to claim even this is to claim too much for the historian. Possibilities cannot be excluded. Not only is it the case that other scholars, now or in the future, may make a different assessment of the existing evidence, but new evidence could be discovered to change our understanding, or even the historicity of the best attested data from the past. Historians cannot 'establish' anything. As far as miracle is concerned a historian, on this argument, could say no more than that an oddity may have occurred.

Two replies are possible. The first is to point out that we have here a commonplace of all human knowledge, except self-authenticating systems in mathematics and logic. Whatever we think we know, something may turn up to upset our confidence; we cannot escape this principle of 'fallibilism'. Knowledge is never absolutely certain. In the second place we are not, in practice, impeded by this rational quagmire. We are perfectly capable of telling when evidence is so strong that we can ignore the theoretical possibility of challenge; we talk of 'being certain' where otherwise we would talk of being 'reasonably sure'. And this applies to history as well as to the rest of life. The weight of evidence that President John F. Kennedy was shot in Dallas, Texas, on 22 November 1963 is so overwhelming that the possibility in logic that persuasive evidence to the contrary could exist can be ignored as a fantasy.[3]

Accounting for the empty tomb

Accepting that the historian can collect and assess data with some hope of reaching a limited but substantive conclusion, how does this apply to the central miracle claimed by Christianity, the resurrection of Jesus Christ? The documentary reliability of the New Testament material has already been discussed. As we have seen, there is no reason to doubt the basic honesty of the records we have, or their direct link with the events themselves, but every reason to doubt their impartiality. The death of Christ by crucifixion at the hands of the Roman authorities seems, therefore, beyond question, confirmed as it is by non-Christian sources.

The precise date is a matter of difficulty and dispute. The month and the day of the week are clear, a Friday in or prior to the festival of Passover which was celebrated on the fourteenth day of the Jewish month of Nisan, the lunar month falling in March/April. The year, however, is less certain. Jewish calendars and liturgical uses in the first century are complicated. What is more, although the Synoptic Gospels put the arrest of Jesus after the Passover meal on the Thursday evening, John appears to say that the Passover meal that year was celebrated on the Friday evening, that is to say, after the crucifixion. The most likely years are 30 and 33 AD.

According to Christian writers, the body of Christ was buried in a rock tomb and placed under guard, but the following Sunday morning it was gone. Christ's followers saw him again, alive, and he continued to appear to them over a period of six weeks. They then waited a week more before beginning to proclaim the resurrection publicly. In terms of what the historian can consider, this story is a claim that the tomb where the body had been placed was found empty and that there is no historical explanation for this, and that Christianity derives from that alleged event.

How, in the first place, should the data be taken? Was the tomb empty? It is hard to argue that it was not. It was open to the authorities to discredit the Christian stories at one blow by producing the corpse. They did not, and instead the Jewish story was that the disciples had stolen the body. It clearly could not be found. We reach a similar conclusion if we reject the New Testament chronology and assume that a longer period elapsed before the preaching of a resurrection began. It would then have been simple for the authorities to 'discover' a convenient skeleton. But they did not, and this must argue that the emptiness of the tomb was established knowledge in Jerusalem.

The problem then becomes this: How could the tomb have been empty? Suggestions that the wrong tomb was examined by the disciples do not stand up; the correct one and the corpse it contained could easily have been pointed out. The idea that the body was secretly removed by the authorities to avoid trouble must also imply that they could later have produced it – which they did not. The theory that Jewish extremists stole the body as an act of defiance piles hypothesis upon hypothesis – that nationalists were involved with Jesus, that they thought him a martyr (and we know that the one disciple with nationalist connections, Judas, thought Jesus a failure), and that the secret disposal of his body would have served their cause. Blaming the disciples will not do either. The notion that they stole or moved the body and conspired to fabricate or at least tolerate a new religion based upon personal integrity and commitment to a risen Christ whom they knew was still dead, beggars belief. Equally far-fetched are theories that the Roman execution squad botched the job so that Jesus of Nazareth was not, when buried, actually dead, and thus he was able to 'revive' in the tomb. In short, a convincing physical explanation of the empty tomb has yet to be suggested.

More promising today would seem to be a psychological explanation, that although his body remained in the tomb, his disciples became convinced that he was really alive. Under the impact of the personality of Jesus and the trauma of the crucifixion, and triggered off by hysterical female visions, the disciples saw what subconsciously they wanted to see. The problem with this explanation is not only the possibility of the authorities preventing the spread of the initial delusions by producing the body, but also the limited period for which these visions were claimed. There is not an infinite series of appearances, only appearances over six weeks. The Christians were left with the awkward problem of asserting that Christ was alive and had appeared to many people but, sorry, he did so no longer.

What is more, a psychological explanation of the resurrection asks a great deal of hallucination. This had to be widespread, sudden and permanent. On its own admission, Christ's circle of followers had collapsed in terror and flight after his arrest, yet as far back as we can get in Christian traditions, there is attached to the resurrection the tag 'the third day'. There is no gradual, spreading sublimation of personal loss into spiritualities, still less a refusal to accept that Christ was really dead. Rather, there is a crude lurch from the defeat of death to a permanent and unshakable conviction of life. As J.G.Davies has written:

> The accounts of the resurrection appearances, impossible though it may be to reconcile them, are evidence that Jesus' followers were convinced that they had seen him risen and had had a personal encounter not with a ghost but with one who had died but was now alive, having broken the power of death.[4]

Any hallucination, indeed, must have been extreme, powerful enough to blind men who were well aware of the literal truth, that Christ's remains were where they always had been. The earliest Christian material, the letters of Paul of Tarsus, come from a man who must, as a former confidant of the Jewish leaders, have known the truth about the tomb. Yet Paul is adamant that 'God raised him from the dead.' Paul had once been sufficiently incensed by the falsity of the resurrection to persecute all who taught it; equally, when he accepted that Christ was alive, this was no conviction of a 'spiritual' resurrection – 'his soul goes marching on' – for Paul based key elements in his thinking on the physical reality of the empty tomb.

The human mind can play tricks, but it is unreasonable to suppose that psychological disturbance can, by itself, account satisfactorily for such a massive determination to ignore the evidence which still lay decomposing in that tomb.

Only a radical solution will escape the impasse of the evidence; either the acceptance that whatever caused the body of Christ to disappear is still, after nearly 2,000 years, without explanation in normal terms, or the rejection of the whole episode as a fabrication, a pious myth in which there is no way of separating legend and reality. The first solution would leave open the possibility which the Christian faith presents, that the events after the crucifixion are not explicable in natural terms because they were supernaturally produced, and this is to pass beyond the boundaries of the historian's competence. The second solution would have to meet the documentary evidence from twenty years after the crucifixion, that preaching of the resurrection was well established in the Eastern Mediterranean at a time and in an area where the facts would still have been known. It would also have to face the evidence that, some thirty years afterwards and as far away as Rome, Christians were ready to die for their beliefs.

The spread of the early church defies the conclusion that nothing happened. Tacitus himself records that the execution of Christ 'checked that pernicious superstition for a short time, but it broke out afresh'.[5] Why should it 'break out afresh', and how could the vital plant of early Christianity have sprung from a root so crushed as the first disciples were by the destruction of their leader? The alternative to leaving the door open for a non-natural explanation is to face the problem of accounting for the appearance of Christianity.

Notes and references

1 A.Robinson, 'Communication' in *Past and Present* 4, 1953, 76.

2 David Hume, *Essays Moral, Political and Literary*, ed. T.H.Green and T.H.Grose, Longmans, Green and Co., 1875, ii.93.

3 The relativist argument, that we can never be certain about anything in the past because any conclusions of historian 'A' will always be liable to be upset by new evidence or a new interpretation from historian 'B', rests upon a logical fallacy. 'B' can only say that 'A' was *definitely wrong* if he is able to establish that what 'A' claimed was *impossible*. To demonstrate this 'B' must produce an argument which cannot later be disproved; this is impossible, since behind 'B' is historian 'C'. To prove that what 'A' wrote was, whatever he claimed, necessarily *uncertain*, we need to argue that 'B' can be *certain*, which is contradictory. The potentiality for conflict and revision in history does not, therefore, reduce all statements to the level of provisional opinion; everything turns on the kind of statement and the weight of the evidence.

4 J.G.Davies, *The Early Christian Church*, Greenwood Press, 1965, p. 28.

5 F.F.Bruce, *Jesus and Christian Origins outside the New Testament*, Hodder and Stoughton, 1974, p. 22.

Chapter 4

One faith among many

The most offensive feature of Christianity is its exclusiveness. A religion whose founder is credited with saying, 'No one comes to the Father except by me' has produced followers who dismiss the religious aspirations of other men as 'heathen blindness'.[1] Such an attitude might be excusable in medieval times when the only other great systems of belief known to the Christian world were Judaism and Islam, belonging with Christianity to the same family of Semitic religions. At least it made sense to argue how the one true God had revealed himself—through Moses, through Christ building on Moses or through Muhammad building on Christ and Moses? But the discovery of the great religions of the East changed all that. Elaborate forms of belief and subtle moral systems from a quite different tradition were discovered to be comparable with and sometimes reminiscent of the supposedly unique insights of Christianity. By the eighteenth century critics of Christianity were saying openly that difference in religion was a matter of culture, not truth. Today the assumption is widespread that all great religions are ultimately the same and vary only in the way metaphysical truths are expressed.

The world of comparative religion is the world of the theologian and the anthropologist, not the historian. But if Christianity takes such a stand upon historical event, the observer is bound to ask whether other faiths are similarly grounded. Is the Christian position unique, as it claims? A comparison can only be made with religions which have, as Christianity does, a specific point of origin. It would be meaningless to check the historical credentials of faiths such as Hinduism and Shinto which do not claim to have started from a special revelation of some kind. As for the founders of Confucianism and Taoism, Kung-fu-tzu (Confucius) and Lao-tzu, we seem to be dealing with masters of philosophy more than originators in religion.

The question does not apply completely to the Jewish religion, either. This claims to have been revealed by God in a sequence of historical events and through a succession of teachers and prophets, a claim which Christianity would in large measure accept. On the other hand, the way revelation is understood in Judaism is different. God's action is principally understood in an appreciation of what events mean; it never takes effect through a person of divine origin. The Spirit of God is certainly seen moving in persons and happenings, but it is not incarnate as a particular individual. The two world faiths which can be compared to Christianity historically, are Islam and Buddhism. Where Christians look to the crucifixion and resurrection in, say AD 30, Muslims look to Muhammad's flight from Mecca in AD 622 and Buddhists to the 'Enlightenment' of Siddhartha Gotama, probably in 528 BC.

Muhammad: Messenger of God

That Islam is the religion of its founder is beyond question. It was no evolving belief and it was no philosophy; the Kalima or Muslim creed declares, 'there is no God but God, and Muhammad is the prophet of God'. He was born about AD 570 at Mecca, and after a deprived childhood married a wealthy widow and worked as a trader. In middle age he became a wandering holy-man and eventually was convinced of a call from God to become a prophet, proclaiming a stern monotheism to the polytheistic tribes of the area. Much of his teaching was derived from Jewish and Christian sources and it is clear that Muhammad expected to be welcomed by both faiths. Only when disappointed in this and faced with widespread hostility from superstitious communities around did the prophet declare a holy war which eventually took his followers to the Pyrenees and to the gates of Vienna.

The message which Muhammad received is recorded in the *Qur'an*, by tradition a transcription of a tablet preserved in heaven and revealed to him progressively by the angel Gabriel. Textual analysis suggests that the book preserves some fragments of the prophet's earliest teaching and that these were first expanded by him into a fuller 'Recital' (*Qur'an*) of his revelations and later augmented by the addition of prepared material. After his death his disciples inserted further matter to produce a complete corpus of Muhammad's teaching.

The principal theme of the *Qur'an* is the revelation of God. This revelation comes from God to man through angels and prophets, and it lays upon man the duty to respond and the knowledge that he will have to answer in person for his response. God is compassionate, the *Qur'an* says, and he will accept and forgive, but the qualities which ring out above all are the oneness and the otherness of God. The title Muhammad used, Allah, is a contraction of *Al-ilāh*, 'the God': again and again he points out that God is infinitely removed from what he has created: 'there is no god but Him; all things shall perish except Himself.'[2] From time to time the *Qur'an* reads like nothing other than a swingeing Old Testament attack upon idolatry and paganism.

The Qur'an and the Old Testament

There is, indeed, a close affinity between Muhammad and the ancient Hebrew prophets. Together they share a burning zeal to proclaim the uniqueness, the holiness and the power of God. The *Qur'an* begins,

> Praise be to God, Lord of Creation, the Compassionate, the Merciful, King of Judgement-day!
>
> You alone we worship, and to You alone we pray for help.
>
> Guide us to the straight path, the path of those You have favoured, not of those who have incurred Your wrath, nor of those who have gone astray.

Psalm 86 declares,

> Among the gods not one is like thee, O Lord,
>   no deeds are like thine.
> All the nations thou hast made, O Lord, will come,
> will bow down before thee and honour thy name;
>   for thou art great, thy works are wonderful,
>   thou alone art God.
>
> Guide me, O Lord,
> that I may be true to thee and follow thy path;
>   let me be one in heart
>   with those who revere thy name.[3]

Like the prophets of the Jewish canon, Muhammad believed in a God who demanded total righteousness from his creatures:

> The worshippers who are steadfast in prayer; who set aside a due portion of their goods for the needy and the dispossessed; who truly believe in the Day of Reckoning and dread the punishment of their Lord; who restrain their carnal desire; who keep their trusts and promises and bear true witness; and who attend to their prayers with promptitude – these shall be laden with honours and shall dwell in fair gardens.

The psalmist asks,

> Who may dwell on the holy mountain?
> The man of blameless life, who does what is right
> and speaks the truth from his heart;
>   who has no malice on his tongue,
> who never wrongs a friend
> and tells no tales against his neighbour;
> the man who shows his scorn for the worthless
> and honours all who fear the Lord;
> who swears to his own hurt and does not retract;
> who does not put his money out to usury
> and takes no bribe against an innocent man.
> He who does these things shall never be brought low.[4]

There is in *Qur'an* and Old Testament alike a concern for the weak and unfortunate, a hatred of exploitation. Where, thirteen hundred years earlier, Amos had scourged those

> who grind the destitute and plunder the humble, you who say, 'When will the new moon be over so that we may sell corn? When will the sabbath be past so that we may open our wheat again, giving short measure in the bushel and taking overweight in the silver, tilting the scales fraudulently and selling the dust of the wheat; that we may buy the poor for silver and the destitute for a pair of shoes?'

Muhammad cried:

> Woe to the unjust who, when others measure for them, exact in full, but when they measure or weigh for others, defraud them!

> The righteous man...for the love of God gives his wealth to his kinsfolk, to the orphans, to the needy, to the wayfarers and to the beggars, and for the redemption of captives.[5]

Muhammad's awareness of himself

This link with earlier prophets is more than a matter of similarity in thought and language; it is fundamental to Muhammad's appreciation of himself and his mission. He saw his task to be the proclamation of a truth which was, as he understood it, the truth taught in the Old Testament and continued by Jesus Christ.

> He has ordained for men the faith He has revealed to you and formerly enjoined on Noah and Abraham, on Moses and Jesus, saying: 'Observe this faith and be united in it'.

Certainly he saw himself as the culmination of this previous witness; the *Qur'an* is the supreme revelation. He had no doubts either about his apostolic precedence and authority; his message was 'if you love God, follow me'. But Muhammad was nevertheless absolute in the conviction that he was not more than a prophet.

> We made a solemn covenant with you as We did with the other prophets; with Noah and Abraham; with Moses and Jesus the son of Mary.

Again and again he insists that he is a mortal, destined to die, and that it is the message which is divine.[6]

The need to assert his own humanity was indeed, an essential consequence of Muhammad's conviction of the total uniqueness of God. The insistence by Christians that Christ was divine therefore seemed to him their great error and the greatest possible blasphemy: 'There is but one God...The Messiah, the son of Mary, was no more than an apostle.' He appears to have understood the Trinity to comprise God the Father, Mary the Mother and Jesus the Son, and he portrays Christ's denial of such a falsehood.

> God will say: 'Jesus, son of Mary, did you ever say to mankind: "Worship me and my mother as gods beside God?" '
>
> 'Glory to You', he will answer, 'How could I say that to which I have no right?'[7]

Muhammad makes it abundantly clear that he himself is no saviour, simply the messenger of the eternal truth about God.

> Say: 'I am no prodigy among the apostles; nor do I know what will be done with me or you. I follow only what is revealed to me, and my only duty is to give plain warning.'
>
> No soul shall bear another's burden. If a laden soul cries out for help, not even a near relation shall share its burden.

It is for this reason that the horror at some of Muhammad's behaviour, traditional in the West, is quite beside the point. He did not pretend to be perfect and apparently felt that as the Prophet he was entitled to certain relaxations in the law, but none of this affects the truth of his message in the slightest. Indeed, in a way it accentuates the truth that glory belongs to God alone;

> Say: I am but a mortal like yourselves. It is revealed to me that

your Lord is one God. Let him that hopes to meet his Lord do what is right and worship none besides Him.[8]

Christianity and Islam

The historical affinity between the origins of Christianity and Islam is obvious – a leader of remarkable personality and insight, the struggle against distortions in current religion, the recruiting of a handful of believers and ultimate triumph as a world force, the preservation of the message in a sacred book. There is a community of background and ideas – the Old Testament, the values of Semitic society, the claim to reveal the one true God. From time to time there is even some parallel in language and idiom. Where Christ said 'love your enemies and pray for your persecutors', Muhammad said, 'requite evil with good and he who is your enemy will become your dearest friend'; the criticism of hypocritical prayer in the Sermon on the Mount is parallelled by, 'Woe to those who pray but are heedless in their prayer; who make a show of piety and give no alms to the destitute'; the last judgement is depicted by Muhammad in very much the terms used by Christ.[9]

Yet although Islam and Christianity have these affinities, they differ in one crucial respect. To the Muslim, Muhammad was a prophet who in a particular time and place proclaimed the eternal truth about God. To the Christian, Jesus of Nazareth was demonstrated through the events of his life, death and resurrection to be the Son of God. It is a contrast between what is taught and the identity of the teacher, between truth preached in a historical situation and truth revealed in a historical person. There is a different relationship to history. The Prophet is supremely important because he brought the supreme revelation from God; Christ is supremely important because he is the supreme revelation, a revelation in a historical phenomenon. Thus the *kerygma* tells of the facts about Christ, the *Qur'an* recites a truth about God.

The contrast is brought out in the names 'Christianity' and 'Islam'. The one comes from the nickname 'Christ's men', the other was adopted by Muhammad and means 'to submit [to God]'; commitment to a person is set against commitment to a revelation of who God is and of what he requires.[10] It is a solecism to speak of a 'Muhammadan', a follower of Muhammad; the proper term is 'Muslim', that is 'a submitting [one]'.

To put the point crudely, if it could be shown that Muhammad had never existed, this would not affect the validity or invalidity of the insights of the *Qur'an* into the nature of God. If Jesus Christ had never existed, the message of Christianity would have been a nonsense from the start, and if his death and resurrection did not take place, the Christian 'good news' is null and void. In the last resort, therefore, Christianity is in a different position to Islam. It stands or falls by its historical reliability; Islam does not.

Buddhism: the problem of the evidence

To turn from Islam to Buddhism is to move from a religion which is naturally comparable to Christianity to one which is, at first sight, remote. It is also to turn from a faith embodied in a written source to a faith which circulated for several centuries in only an oral form. The reason for this is not the antiquity of Buddhism; this originated in the late sixth century BC, in Western terms in the generation before Socrates and Plato, and is less ancient than much of the Old Testament. The message remained an oral one because it was preserved by the *Sangha* or Buddhist monastic order where each generation of monks taught it to the next. It was not until the first century BC that written texts were made, when, according to tradition, the monks, 'since they saw that the people were falling away, met together, and in order that the true doctrine might endure, wrote it down in books'.[11]

This by itself would raise severe problems in form criticism for anyone trying to recover the original Buddhist message, but a further complication arises from the divisions among Buddhists which began within a century of the 'Enlightenment'. In particular there is the major rift between Theravada Buddhism, 'the teaching of the elders', and the more speculative Mahayana schools. Since these divisions were well established by the time the scriptures were reduced to writing, different schools of monks recorded different material. There is, in consequence, no accepted canon and no single acknowledged text of the Buddha's teaching. As Edward Conze has written:

> Buddhist tradition differs fundamentally from that of Christianity. In Christianity we can distinguish an 'initial tradition', embodied in the New Testament from a 'continuing tradition', which consists of the Fathers and doctors of the Church, the decisions of councils and synods, and the pronouncements of various hierarchies. Buddhists possess nothing that corresponds to the New Testament. The 'continuing tradition' is all that is clearly attested.[12]

Given these problems, we have no hope of exploring the origins of Buddhism in the detail possible for Christianity and Islam. Nevertheless we can establish the main lines of the story. Particularly in the Pali Canon, the scriptures of the Theravada school, we are close to what was taught by the founder's early disciples and we are as near as we can get to some of his actual words.

Siddhartha, 'the Enlightened One'

Siddhartha was born in 563 BC or thereabouts, into the Gotama family, a clan belonging to the tribal aristocracy of the Shakyas of Southern Nepal. Late accounts describe his father as a king or rajah, but he was more probably the chief citizen of Kapilavastu, the principal city of the Shakyas, a town on the trade route which skirted the foothills of the Himalaya. It was an urban background and a status which was to allow Gotama to move freely in the society of the Ganges plain. What led him to break with the life he was born to and ultimately to become a peripatetic teacher was an overwhelming sense of the frustration and sorrow of life. His awareness of this is symbolized for later biographers by the story of his meeting first an old man, then a sick man and then a corpse, and receiving each time in answer to his question 'Why?', the refrain, 'This comes to all men'.

Finding no release in asceticism Gotama turned to deliberate analysis of the human condition, aided by the disciplines of meditation. The result was the breakthrough that is called 'the Enlightenment'. This, by tradition, took place when Gotama was about thirty-five years old and after a period of deliberate and strenuous meditation under a fig tree at Buddh Gaya, 150 miles/240 km east of Benares. At that point he became 'the Buddha', 'the Enlightened One', a title which Buddhists reserve for anyone who has achieved this full illumination of the meaning of existence but which belongs particularly to Gotama. He preached his new understanding and soon had a growing band of disciples whom he organized into the *Sangha* which is named after the body of elders or nobles who governed the Shakya and other clans.

Suffering and the human ego

To understand something of what the Enlightenment was, we need to understand what Gotama meant by suffering. This was not casual unhappiness or misfortune but the consequence of change and decay which is inherent in all things. Nothing is permanent. How then can happiness be real when we know that it cannot last? How can one man even rejoice in a fortunate pleasure when he knows that his fellows are unfortunate? Nor is death an ultimate release from the human malaise; the Buddha accepted the common Indian view that existence was a migration from one life to another in an ever-recurring process of reincarnation. This was the consequence of *karma*, the self-evident fact that reaction follows action, effect follows cause, harvest follows sowing; birth results from the dynamic built up in previous existences. Man is bound to an endless belt of suffering.

How was the chain of consequence to be broken? Not by asceticism, the Buddha decided; he had tried that. To eliminate suffering it was necessary to determine the cause, and this he declared to be desire for permanent individuality. It is this grasping after the ego which continually replenishes the weight of *karma* and so condemns man to frustration. This is the substance of the first two of the 'Four Noble Truths' which sum up the Enlightenment. The third truth provides the remedy. Cessation from suffering follows cessation of desire, and desire ceases when we accept the lust for an independent existence for what it is, a delusion. The ego is as impermanent as the rest of phenomena and not until we accept this will the thrust of *karma* begin to diminish and progress start towards the eventual cessation of all passion and all rebirth, *nirvana*. How we can strip away the self is the theme of the fourth truth, the 'Eightfold Path' of morality, meditation and the attainment of wisdom.

What is absent from the teaching of Gotama is any reference to any deity. On the existence or non-existence of an ultimate reality he maintained a 'noble silence', which we can call 'positive' agnosticism. If the ultimate is ultimate, then it cannot be known and metaphysical speculation is pointless, or worse, for it distracts us from the human condition which is the real concern: would a man wounded by an arrow be wise to bother about the make of the bow?

What Gotama offers is a way of personal salvation, but the ground is humanism and the means, reason. He makes no claim to prophetic vision in the way Muhammad does. Indeed his message is the truth because he has achieved the correct analysis, not because he is proclaiming dogma; 'I am an analyst, not a dogmatist', he said, and he expected his hearers to criticise his dialectic. He claimed nothing of himself which could not be true of other men eventually and, like other men, accepted that he would die.

Seeing whatever is brought into being contains within itself the inherent necessity of dissolution, how can it be that such a being (as the visible Gotama) should not be dissolved?

He rejected the idea of a saviour – 'Look not for refuge to anyone' – and his last words were:

> Behold now, O monks, I exhort you, saying, All component things must grow old. Work out your own salvation with diligence.

His teaching would be left behind, but his own state after death offered them no supernatural grace:

> It is inept to say of the Attainer of the Supernal that after dying the Buddha is or is not, or both is and is not, or neither is nor is not.[13]

A critique of individuality

To the majority of men, especially in the West, the notion that individuality must wither away in order to find peace has appeared the peace of annihilation. Admittedly it is akin to the relief following the removal of an aching tooth, but it is hard to see what remains to enjoy the absence of pain. It is here that the difficulty of getting behind the teaching of the elders is a particular disadvantage. The Theravada school may have exaggerated the pessimistic tendency in the Buddha's teaching and some scholars have seen in the earliest texts a hint that he accepted the belief that *nirvana* was union with the unknowable ultimate: certainly he denied that he taught annihilation.

More important, however, than speculation as to what he may or may not have taught about the nature of *nirvana* is the implication of the Buddha's criticism of individuality for life here and now. If the sovereign ego is an illusion, it follows that it cannot be a satisfactory basis for life, either for the individual or the community. The Buddha's teaching is, of necessity, a call to a radically new, non-individualistic society. This has only recently been recognized in the West and is one of the great positive features to set against the pessimism in Buddhism. It is seen especially in the ideals of the *Sangha* where the monk does not even own his begging bowl and where the whole atmosphere is intended to free men from concern for themselves. Outside the order, the laity are offered a blueprint for modest, moral living in which mutual dependence and responsibility replaces self-assertion. It is not surprising that questioning of the virtues of individualism in the West has been accompanied by increased interest in Gotama's ideas.

Christianity and Theravada Buddhism

If the Buddha is one of the world's great religious thinkers and if the essence of his thought is the reduction of unbridled individuality by rational methods, the contrasts with Jesus Christ are obvious. Although each saw the human self as crucial, the good news offered by the Buddha is the antithesis of the good news offered by the Christ. In one case we are offered a way to save ourselves, in the other a way to be saved; the goal of perfection in *nirvana* is set against the goal of perfection in Christ. But for the historian, the important difference is that Buddhism does not have the appeal to events which is basic to Christianity.

What is supreme in Buddhism is the teaching. As Edward Conze has written:

> Unlike official Christianity, Buddhism is not a historical religion and its message is valid independently of the historicity of any event in the life of the 'founder' who did not found anything, but merely transmitted a Teaching pre-existing him since eternity.

It is no accident that in the earliest Buddhist material there is a marked concentration upon the teaching of its founder and not upon his life. Biographical interest only becomes considerable after the turn of the second century. Edward Conze even goes so far as to say that 'the existence of Gotama as an individual is a matter of little importance to the Buddhist faith'. As with Islam, Buddhism is historical in the sense that it had a specific origin in history, but it is not historical in the sense that it stands or falls by the facts of its origin.[14]

Christianity, Islam and Buddhism (in its initial form) are the three great religious systems which arose in known historical contexts and from the impulse of known founders. The student of religion might set the agnosticism of the last against the theism of the other two; a sociologist might pair the Christian church and the Buddhist *Sangha*. In historical terms it is Christianity which is the odd-man-out. As H.D.Lewis has said:

> Christianity has the Jesus of History at the centre of it. It is a position he is never to vacate. This is the radical difference between Christianity and other religions which have much in common with it.[15]

The 'good news' about the 'Anointed One' stands against the message of 'the Prophet' and the wisdom of 'the Enlightened One'.

The God-Man syndrome

We have examined the claim that the stand of Christianity upon history is unique among the world's religions. But there is a further aspect of the alleged distinctiveness of the Christian faith which must also be mentioned briefly. Granted that Christianity appeals to historical fact in a way other faiths do not, is it true that the interpretation which it places on those facts is also without parallel? Belief in an incarnate god is found in other religions as well. In the deification of the historical Christ are we seeing more than a common phenomenon in religious history?

Divine incarnation is a prominent concept in Hinduism, a religion which has not concerned us hitherto. To Western observers, popular Hinduism may appear to be a welter of polytheistic superstition, but an instructed Hindu will argue that we need to see in these cults and mythologies an attempt to express an ultimate reality, *Brahman*. K.M.Sen insisted:

> We must remember that in the Hindu philosophy there is no contradiction between belief in an all-embracing, all-pervading omnipresent God and worship of a variety of gods and goddesses of the Hindu pantheon. In religious ceremonies the images of gods may help to focus devotion, but in theory they represent nothing more than imaginative pictures of the infinite aspects of one all-pervading God.[16]

Some Hindu thought claims that all existence is one (monism). From this standpoint the world is either a manifestation of the universal *Brahman*, or (in a more extreme view) an illusion, *Brahman* being the only reality. For the monist of either persuasion, the conclusion is that man's higher self is one with the *Brahman*, a view summed up in the aphorism, 'Thou art That'. An alternative position (dualism) suggests that some real distinction can be drawn between the self and reality, and very generally conceives of that reality in personal terms. Thus monism envisages a supreme abstraction, dualism a supreme person. And a supreme person may reveal himself in finite shape, that is, he can become incarnate.

The avatars of Vishnu

For the Hindu dualist, incarnation of the supreme being is a characteristic of his manifestation as the god Vishnu. Vishnu the Preserver is said to have made ten (or twenty-four) 'descents' or *avatars* to protect the universe from calamity. Not all were in human form. As a boar he rooted up the earth from the depths of the ocean; in the guise of a fish he intervened to save humanity from the Flood. The concept is, however, most developed in the identification of Vishnu with the hero-king Rama and with Krishna 'the Blessed One', a prince and charioteer.

The legend of Rama dates, perhaps, from the fifth century BC and in its early forms clearly presents Rama as a mortal ruler. But the *Ramayana*, or 'Adventures of Rama', was reworked into a book of devotion presenting Rama as the *avatar* of Vishnu. Krishna appears in the other great Indian epic, the *Mahabharata* or 'Wars of the Great Barata Family'. This is now the longest epic in the world, but the earliest part, only some 10 per cent of the final version, depicts Krishna as a minor warrior. In later additions, notably the *Bhagavad Gita*, he becomes an *avatar* of Vishnu and expounds a gospel of good works and divine grace.

The contrast between the incarnation of Christ and the incarnations of Vishnu is obvious. In one we have a single once-for-all manifestation of God which exists together with a full humanity. In the other we have a series of 'discontinuous incarnations' in which the god takes on the form of a man or animal. The Christian concept is that of divine self-limitation, where Jesus 'empties' himself of the glory to which he is entitled in order to be born, live and communicate fully as a man among men. Only at the 'transfiguration' was that glory ever apparent, and this was an isolated instance, experienced in secret by three close friends. By contrast the divinity of the Hindu *avatar* is never far below the surface. Krishna's mother opens her son's mouth and sees the whole universe; he terrifies the warrior Arjuna with the full blaze of deity; grappling in the river with the hydra Kaliya, the god sees his fellow villagers terrified:

> Not knowing who he really was, they thought that his death had come ... Krishna, seeing that his own village, with its women and children, was so miserable because of him ... conformed to the way of mortals and, staying for a moment, rose up from the serpent's grip. The serpent ... tortured by the expanding body of Krishna, released him.[17]

Not only are there differences between Hindu and Christian conceptions of incarnation, there is also the historical difference. Krishna and Rama are historical figures in only a remote sense, (they may be based on some actual person, we cannot be certain), and there is no question of the incarnations of Vishnu referring to specific events in the historical past. In Christianity, however, the divinity of Christ was a conclusion wrung from monotheistic Jews

in their attempt to describe the identity of one particular man.
A.C.Bouquet put the matter well:

> It must be borne in mind that the doctrine of the incarnation in
> orthodox Christian theology is not an expression of a myth in
> theological form, but an attempt to codify and express a real
> historical experience, namely the impact of the genuine
> historical personality and career of Jesus of Nazareth upon the
> world of men and women.[18]

The Divine Buddha

One concept of incarnation which remains to be considered is that
of the Mahayana school of Buddhists. This has moved away from
the agnosticism of Gotama's thinking and, instead, sees him as an
incarnation of the divine. This change came about, in part, under
the influence of Hindu notions of *avatars* which ultimately
pronounced the Buddha an appearance of Vishnu, but its most
numerous adherents are in China and Tibet, not India. Theravada
Buddhism is now the minority form and survives only in Sri Lanka
and parts of South-East Asia. In Mahayana Buddhism, the
Buddha has ceased to be a human teacher and has become, instead, a divine saviour. He is worshipped as the manifestation of
the supreme deity and supported by a pantheon of lesser Buddhas.

Some writers have suggested a parallel between this divine
Buddha who came to earth to save men and is now glorified, and
the Christian vision that Christ, in the words of the creed,
'ascended into heaven and sits at the right hand of God'. But the
similarity is superficial; the Mahayana incarnation is as far away
from Christ's incarnation as the Hindu *avatars* are. Instead of increasing the importance of Gotama as a figure in history,
Mahayana Buddhism has reduced it. The more the Buddha has
been seen in the lights of divinity, the less important have the
human facts appeared to be. This tendency is also accentuated by
the belief that ultimate reality has manifested itself in more than
one Buddha. J.B.Pratt expressed the point like this: 'Other
religions have made their founders into gods and sons of God;
Buddhism makes its founders into the Ultimate and Only Reality.'
And in the future lies the hope of Maitreya, the Buddha yet to
come. T.R.V.Murti is emphatic:

> In Mahayana, though Gautama is a historical person, he is not
> the only Buddha, and his occurrence is *one* of the innumerable
> acts of divine dispensation. The Mahayana religion escapes the

predicament of having to depend on any one particular historical person and the founder of its religion.[19]

The divine Buddha is a revered historical figure who was transmuted into a god after time had weakened the pull of the empirical evidence. Thus Mahayana incarnation recedes from the historical event; Christian incarnation is a hypothesis to account for the historical event. It may be possible to draw theological parallels between Christianity and Buddhism in the Mahayana form; parallels in history there are not.

The Same or Different?

Once the eyes of the Christian world had been opened to the religions of the East, exclusive assumptions and attitudes hallowed by centuries were called in question. More than this, Christianity seemed to be reduced to a religion among other religions. The consequence has been that people have begun to search for universal principles in belief and a common denominator for man's experience of the transcendent. Yet distinctiveness is not less important than similarity; a mouse and an elephant can each be described as a four-footed mammal with a nose, ears and a tail. We wrong the integrity of Muhammad, Buddha and Christ when we reduce them to three holy men who said very much the same; the assumption that all faiths, including the Christian faith, are much-of-a-muchness is simply untrue.

As far as Christianity is concerned, and without wishing to restore its aggressive triumphalism, we have to recognise that we are dealing with a religion which is distinct in historical terms. It is not adequately defined as the European manifestation of mankind's search for meaning and for the ultimate. To quote H.D.Lewis again:

> The unique events narrated in the Gospels are the core of the Christian faith. These are not to be taken as mere symbols of something beyond them, whether in the depths of our own experience or in the absolute being of God. They are not just pictures, but supreme religious reality. The Christian faith... stands or falls with the insistence that it was God himself, in the form of a man, who trod this earth two thousand years ago and died between two thieves on a cross. This may not be an acceptable view, and no one should minimize the stark difficulty of it. But it is in fact the essential Christian belief.

Or as Paul said of himself and his fellow believers, 'We proclaim Christ – yes, Christ nailed to a cross'.[20]

Notes and references

1 John 14:6; 'The heathen in his blindness bows down to wood and stone', Reginald Heber, 1819.

2 *The Koran*, ed. N.J.Dawood, Penguin Books, 4th edn. 1974, p. 82; in the following 'Allah' is rendered as 'God'.

3 *ibid*. p. 15; Psalm 86:8–11.

4 *Koran* p. 58; Psalm 15.

5 Amos 8:4–6; *Koran* pp. 49, 350.

6 *ibid*. pp. 155, 410, 290.

7 *ibid*. pp. 395, 400.

8 *ibid*. pp. 127, 179–80, 100.

9 Matthew 5:44; *Koran* pp. 161, 28.

10 'Christian' was a Greek nickname coined when the church came into contact with Gentile society. Earlier Jewish usage, however, confirms that even then the person of Christ was central to Christian thinking. Within the primitive church the term 'the Way' was used, relating directly to Christ's call to men to 'follow' him and his claim to be 'the Way' [Matthew 8:22 etc.; John 14:6]. Orthodox Jews used the term 'the Nazarenes' which may have begun in an identification of Christians with existing sects of 'observant' (Nazarene) Jews or with the custom of religious separation ('Nazarite' vows), but soon came to mean the followers of Jesus of Nazareth, Jesus the Nazarene.

11 C.Humphreys, *Buddhism*, Penguin Books, 1951, p. 233.

12 *Buddhist Scriptures*, ed. E.Conze, Penguin Books, 1959, p. 11.

13 T.Ling, *The Buddha*, M.T.Smith, 1973, p. 115; Humphreys, *Buddhism*, p. 40; *Buddhist Texts through the Ages,* ed. E.Conze, Harper and Row, 1964, p. 106.

14 E.Conze, *Buddhist Thought in India*, Allen and Unwin, 1962, p. 232; E.Conze, *Buddhism: its Essence and Development* Cassirer, 3rd edn. 1957, p. 34.

15 H.D.Lewis and R.L.Slater, *The Study of Religion*, Penguin Books, 1969, p. 210.

16 K.M.Sen, *Hinduism*, Penguin Books, 1961, p. 35.

17 ed. W.D.O'Flaherty, *Hindu Myths*, Penguin Books, 1975. p. 224f.

18 A.C.Bouquet, *Comparative Religion*, Penguin Books, 1962, p. 135.

19 J.B.Pratt, *The Pilgrimage of Buddhism,* Macmillan, 1928, p. 249; T.R.V.Murti, *The Central Philosophy of Buddhism,* Allen and Unwin, 1960, p. 287.

20 Lewis and Slater, *The Study of Religion*, p. 208; 1 Corinthians 1:23.

Chapter 5

Patterns of the past

For centuries after the dawn of the Christian era, the Western historian automatically began his consideration of the past with the foundation of the world. Even though his main concern was with later happenings, the monk would still trace the revelation of God, first to the Jews and then through the supreme event of human history, the incarnation of Jesus Christ. All else was conceived of as an appendix to this. Few historians would now attempt a universal theme and fewer still would write theocentric history, yet the Christian still assumes that all historical enquiry goes to make up a greater whole and that a historian should be able to perceive the larger pattern. Nor is his expectation unique. Many of the strains of thought which have united with the Christian tradition to make history what it is today, have reinforced the feeling that the subject should offer general syntheses of human experience. The faith of Lord Acton in the possibility of writing 'ultimate' history is out of fashion, but many historians have the conscious, and still more the unconscious feeling that they are contributing to 'the understanding of the past'.

The need for patterns

To accept that there is a long term coherence in history does not, however, oblige the historian to undertake anything so practical as a publisher's contract. He has a horror of generalizing beyond his expertise and, perhaps, a secret fear of what might happen if he tries to put his vision into words. The public, however, are impatient. The professional may prefer to eschew explanations and patterns, but the point made by Voltaire still stands: 'If all you have to tell us is that one barbarian succeeded another barbarian on the banks of the Oxus or Jaxartes, what benefit have you conferred upon the public?'[1]

He is right. What is it which keeps the study of history among the concerns which are proper to occupy a human being when the race as a whole is burdened with the immediate concerns of the

belly? It is, surely, the need to have man's present displayed objec-
tively, that is to have what the individual knows from his own
experience, put in relation to and in perspective with the past; to
show the 'now' for what it is by setting it against the 'then'; to
show how the 'then' relates to the 'now'; to show how mankind
has behaved as a social animal in the thousands of years which lie
before the sixty or seventy years of our own personal existence; to
show how change has happened; these are the purposes, the *raisons
d'être*, of history. And the very notion of history as a subject with
this utility presupposes explanation and pattern – not necessarily
causation, but certainly relationship and perspective.

If, despite the widespread reluctance of historians to consider
the proposition, it is sound to argue that explanation and pattern
are of the essence of history, it is obviously necessary to take the
matter further. And getting the patterns right is not an academic
question. Hitler founded the Third Reich upon historical
generalizations about the Aryan race and the inferiority of non-
Teutonic peoples. A powerful influence upon the United States of
America has been the assumption that it had a 'manifest destiny'.
The appeal to an authentication in history is a strong one. By what
criteria, then, are broad interpretations to be judged? Which are
legitimate, which not? And what of Christian interpretations?

Patterns and presumptions

One suggestion is that there are two different levels of explanation
and pattern. What can be called 'first order' patterns are broad,
general and have to do with the overall progression and interpretation of human events; 'second order' explanations are those
which are made in the course of studying specific historical
problems and periods.

We might suggest for example, that within nineteenth century
British history it is possible to see a trend towards increasing
parliamentary government; this would be a second order pattern.
We might also argue that this is part of a tide in British history,
setting towards liberty, representative institutions and democracy;
this would be a first order pattern. To most historians the former
would be unexceptionable; the latter quite the reverse. It is, indeed, an example of the fallacy in history which can crop up
anywhere, but which we label 'Whig' after those historians who
wrote to demonstrate that the Victorian constitution was the
apotheosis of British history. It is the attitude of the historian who
'organizes his scheme of history from the point of view of his own
day'.[2] He sees the past in terms of progress and reaction, accor-

ding to the contribution to the predestined goal; he approaches history with bland confidence in his own inbuilt presumptions. The sheer distortion of such an approach is as obvious in the erudition of Arnold J.Toynbee as in the ignorance of a prominent British post-war politician who claimed that the victory of parliament over Charles I in 1646 was an early triumph for the Labour Movement.

Must we then assume that the historian is restricted to second order patterns and that he has no justification for claiming the right to offer anything more? If so, no general explanation in Christian terms is legitimate and separation of the historian's faith from his discipline becomes unavoidable.

The dangers of whiggery are real, yet it is not wholly valid to separate in this way the explanations which the historian can give from those which he cannot. It is, rather, the nature of all second order, 'particular', patterns to become first order, 'general', patterns. For one thing, the distinction of 'first' and 'second' seems to depend upon the very strong sense of 'period' which modern historians have developed. The survival of 1485 as a boundary date in British history, despite its known lack of significance, is a good example of its usefulness to the scholar. By starting with the accession of Henry Tudor the historian of the sixteenth century can treat the years before 1485 selectively and briefly, selecting, from the safety of Tudor England, such matters as he considers his readers should notice or that suit his purpose.

Chopping up history into separate periods is a device to escape the horrid reality that history has a pattern and development, if only a chronological one. For, once it is admitted that history is an ongoing continuity, the isolation of first and second order patterns begins to break down. Even should there be a historian strong-minded enough to succeed in avoiding, in the words of a modern text-book, 'themes and analyses, interpretations and Olympian views', his very silence will present a pattern to the reader of his book.[3] 'History', he will be saying, 'is a continuum of events which is random.' In the words attributed to H.A.L.Fisher, 'history is one damn fact after another'.

Another point which makes nonsense of the distinction between second and first order patterns is that history deals with people. The historian who reflects upon the past is forced to employ assumptions about the importance (or otherwise) of human beings and about human nature which are anything but short-term. Indeed, the main reason why he applies these assumptions to the past is the conviction that 'people do behave like that', or 'events happen like that'. The good historian will try to allow for differences which are revealed by contemporary evidence, especially as anthropologists have shown how diverse cultural patterns can be. But the very possibility of understanding the past, that ultimate assumption in history, presumes a general continuum in human society and human behaviour.

For example, a study of the way in which order was maintained in England in the period 1500 to 1700 necessarily involves assumptions about human responses which are assumptions about mankind in general: how people react to social pressure, what power in society is, how ideas and thoughts affect behaviour, how ideas are controlled and disseminated, and so on. To hold that religion was then a means to keep men in obedience is to state a truth about the potential of religion at large.

The human element in history, no less than the time quotient, imposes upon the historian the requirement to offer explanations of the past at a general level, not merely within narrowly specialized definitions. A historian cannot properly fulfil his calling without some overall view of history. We should think poorly of a naturalist who confined himself to dissecting a newly hatched tadpole and never mentioned the frog.

The consequence for the historian who is also a Christian must be exposure of what he believes; no longer can he hug to himself a private understanding of the past. Whatever his faith accepts will produce his pattern for history. If he accepts a God who is supreme, then the will of God must underlie all history. If he accepts a God who is just, then the justice of God must inform all past human experience. That this presents problems is immaterial to the argument; a historian must admit his personal framework for the past and be prepared to justify it.

Patterns justified and unjustified

It may, however, be objected that explanation of the past in terms of the actions of God is outside the province of the historian in much the same way that miracle is. Supernatural considerations are beyond the reference of the subject. Some help may be gained here from the principal group of historians who show no embarrassment at the idea of a general pattern in the past, those who accept the analysis of Karl Marx. For a historian who does so, the English Civil War was an actual class conflict and is also an example of a recurrent pattern of conflict in history which will one day lead to an ultimate classless society.

The appeal of this general hypothesis is its rooting within

history, not in some philosophical assumption; the assertion is that history does work in this particular way. This suggests a test for general explanations of the past: patterns can be divided into those which arise from within the subject and those that are imposed from without. We should think in terms of legitimate, intrinsic explanations which are within the parameters of historical study, and extrinsic, illegitimate explanations which are not. On this distinction, Marxism would fall into the former category; it claims to be an analysis of what goes on in human affairs. The Whig theory, on the other hand, would fall into the second category; it springs from the assumptions the historian brings to the subject and presumes that the present is the necessary consequence of the past.

The great advantage of this formulation is that it makes possible some criterion of proof in history, identifying those generalizations which history can establish and those it cannot. Thus the claim that history demonstrates the superiority of the Aryan race can be tested and shown to be without merit. The assertion that history demonstrates the working of 'progress' (or other Whig virtues) can be shown to be non-historical since everything depends on the way progress is defined, in other words on the subjective assumption that this or that is 'progress'.

Where, on this distinction, does a Christian view of history stand? The answer must be, on both sides. It is extrinsic in claiming a judgement on and a direction of history by God who is outside history. If Alice had stood on the platform of a model railway she could not have determined whether the power supply and the points were being operated by a human controller or a mechanical programmer; in order to know, she would have had to leave Wonderland and observe the system from outside. Similarly, in order for us to identify activity by God we would need to have some external observation point.

The Christian view of history is also an intrinsic one. Like Marxism, it claims that certain factors operate in history, that history does work in a particular way. It must therefore be prepared to argue the case on the evidence. To revert to the model railway; it would have been perfectly possible for Alice to have pondered the running pattern of the trains past her platform and asked what this implied. The implications that follow from this will be considered in the next two chapters.

Patterns and prejudices

There is, however, a further problem which cannot be ignored in any consideration of historical patterning of the past. Deliberately chosen patterns are one thing, but what of the involuntary ones? The broad conspectus of attitudes, assumptions, values and prejudices which influence the approach to life of any individual also influence the historian. Why does he choose the subject he does? How does he formulate this, and what approach does he use? Which sources does he see as specially significant? On none of these questions can the historian be a purely disinterested, rational observer. Most of all, a historian's values will be exposed at the point of his final conclusions. What range of explanations will he admit? What importance will he give to personality, what to 'forces'? The examination paper asks: 'What was the significance of...?' but does not expect discussion of 'significance' *per se*; indeed, the question is normally qualified in an attempt to make such a discussion inappropriate, but in doing so it ducks the fundamental issue. Significance depends in part upon an individual's scale of values.

This is not, of course, peculiar to history or even to the humanities. Nor is it confined to those who admit a religious or political commitment; believer, unbeliever, pagan, Christian, atheist, agnostic, Marxist, humanist, liberal, reactionary – all degrees of the philosophical compass produce different points of view. Nor is it possible to hide behind scholarly detachment or attempted objectivity. A historian's presumptions and his selection and handling of material must produce a pattern.

The classic example of this was the work of H.A.L.Fisher. The preface to his *History of Europe* explains that he cannot see 'a plot, a rhythm, a predetermined pattern' in history, 'only one emergency following upon another as wave follows upon wave'. But this same preface shows that for Fisher the theme of history was progress, not progress in a linear but in a tidal manner.

> The fact of progress is written plain and large on the page of history; but progress is not a law of nature. The ground gained by one generation may be lost by the next. The thoughts of men may flow into the channels which lead to disaster and barbarism.... After gaining ground through the nineteenth century, the tides of liberty have now [1936] suddenly receded over wide tracts of Europe.[4]

Willy-nilly, private patterns will show. And so they should. The only defence the reader has is in knowing the direction in which a historian's preconceptions have modified his account. And in any case, they are inevitable. 'A human being is normal with neuroses, not without them'; a historian is normal with a view of life, not without one.

But if we admit this, do we not abandon all claim to verity in history? Does not the subject disintegrate into a relativist swamp of personal opinion? By no means. To go that far would be to accept that there is nothing but personal preference in the writing of history, an argument which is frequently heard but is simply untrue. As we have already seen, the only absolute in history is the evidence, but it is an absolute. The subjectivity of the historian is always controlled by the objective reality of the sources. One scholar may instinctively feel that an episode has been mis-understood, but this remains a private 'hunch' until he makes a case on the evidence. To revert to the philosophical compass; viewpoints will differ but what is in view is still the same.

There is no force, either, in the common contention that evidence is not evidence until it is nominated as such by the historian, and that it is the historian who chooses what are to be the facts. Certainly it is the individual who selects this material and excludes that, who assigns significance to one point and in-significance to another. But he always does this against the totality of what has survived from the past and against the menace of his colleagues who are always free to argue that his selection misleads and his significances are unjustified. It is noticeable that few historians who argue for extreme relativism practise what they profess. They write as though men can understand the past by the rational handling of the evidence. The conclusion must be that total relativism is an entertaining speculation, worth as much serious attention as the possibility that other people exist only in my imagination. Certainly we must recognize a measure of subjec-tivity in every historian, but not that history itself is absolutely subjective.

The need for commitment

What does this mean for the Christian who is also a historian? It means that he need have no shyness about personal commitment colouring his studies. He is not alone. He has no reason to apologize or to bend over backwards to compensate for the values he has. A historian must be honest, not distorting the evidence; he must be fair to the past, not judging by anachronistic standards; he must be true to the discipline of the subject, not arrogating to himself a prophetic mantle. But he need not strain to be neutral, cost what it may. Far from it.

The poet Coleridge once remarked that the historian has 'to

throw himself back' into the past. We have seen the autonomy of history; whatever occurred, occurred, and whatever record it has left, it has left – we cannot add or subtract one iota. We have also seen that it is only possible to understand the past on the assumption that we share a common humanity with previous generations of men and women, that we are one of a kind. Thus, if we want to understand their past we need to bring ourselves. The dry bones of archive material can be arranged into a skeleton by diligent pedantry; they will come alive only if we breath our life into them.

We bring to this task, first, our experience. The greatest study of monasticism in England was undertaken by the late David Knowles. His work is outstanding not because it is bulky, not because of its wide and careful learning, but because Dom David's own religious experience and awareness engendered a warm understanding of the monks of the medieval church, good and bad alike. Nor was experience all he brought, nor is it all we need. We are the same as our ancestors and we are different, and to appreciate the difference we need imagination. Imagination is not invention; the historian does not write fiction. But imagination alone will enable us to enter into the circumstances of other men and women, our predecessors as much as our contemporaries. What is more, only to the informed imagination will the sources yield up their patterns.

Spinoza said that the task of history is not to mock, not to despise, not to lament the actions of men, but to understand them. He is correct only in that the need to understand comes above all else and that condescension is fatal to it. Understanding must demand involvement. Passionate awareness should inform the writer of history, awareness of injustice in society, of the strength and weakness of human character, of the evils of war, of the spirit of man in conflict with its physical, social and mental environment. Appeasement is no qualification for the historian and least of all for the historian who is a Christian. Unless he shivers in the snow with Francis Xavier, desperate to bring Christ to China, unless he charges with Cromwell's Ironsides for God and Parliament, unless he is shamed, with Sitting Bull, before the superior technology, lies and whisky of the God-fearing white man, he is a eunuch.

Notes and references
1 Voltaire, *The Age of Louis XIV and other selected writings*, ed. J.H.Brumfitt, Dent, 1966, p. 333.
2 H.Butterfield, *The Whig Interpretation of History,* Penguin Books, 1975, p. 19.
3 I.Collins, *The Age of Progress*, E.Arnold, 1964, p.v.
4 H.A.L.Fisher, *History of Europe*, E.Arnold, 1936, p.v.

Chapter 6

Destiny and morality:
a world with a plan?

By tradition the Jewish sacred writings are grouped into three, the Law, the Writings and the Prophets. To non-Jews familiar with the Old Testament it is strange to discover that the main historical books found there, the narratives of the Jewish people – Joshua, Samuel, David, Solomon and the rest – are categorized as prophecy. This puts very precisely the Jewish tradition of history. Human events declare to man the actions of God. This is also the Christian tradition; Christ spoke of 'dates and times' being within God's control, and the early Christian writers follow him.

In origin, this belief arises not from a scrutiny of history, but from a study of God. If God is at once supreme and involved in the world, the one who has created it and continues to sustain its existence, then the world and human society must reflect his purpose. More than this, both Jews and Christians believe that God is involved in the world not only in a general sense as creator and preserver, but specifically also in a great plan for human redemption (whether in national terms or in terms of the incarnation of Christ). Human history, therefore, must have a specific direction, something expressed in the concept of the 'coming of the Day of the Lord', the final glory of God in history.

Similarly, if God is creator and sustainer, then the world will, of necessity, reflect his moral character, his justice, both in the way it ought to be organized and conducted and in what follows if that order is disturbed. It is impossible to conceive of a moral deity who has called a morally neutral order of creation into existence. 'The Day of the Lord' is 'the Day of Judgement'. In other words, what Jews and Christians believe about God leads to a belief in a divine purpose and a morality in history.

Consequences within history

Clearly nothing thus far is within the competence of historical criticism; it is extrinsic to history. As Robert Bolton remarked, writing in about 1618:

Christian authors, while for their ease they shuffled up the reasons of events in briefly referring all cause immediately to the Will of God, have generally neglected to inform their readers in the ordinary means of carriage in human affairs and thereby maimed their narratives.[1]

But viewed in another way, destiny and morality are vulnerable to the historian because each alleges a consequence within human affairs; the cause may be outside history, but the effect is in historical events. Quite simply, if the extrinsic claims are to receive any respect as religious statements, it must be possible to show that at the intrinsic level they are not nonsensical.

The importance of demonstrating this is emphasized by the weight which the Bible puts upon the role of God in history. Belief in purpose and belief in a moral universe are not accretions to the main stream of its message, but implicit in the very essence of Christianity.

The purpose of God in human history is a constant theme of the Old Testament. Especially prominent is the concept which the Jews had of a particular destiny for their nation, and, in consequence, their view of history in which each episode was seen as God's response to Israel's needs. But the canon of the Old Testament offers more than this. It also proclaims a God who rules all peoples and a God who speaks in history to all peoples. Isaiah sees the power of Assyria executing the punishment of God and in turn being punished by him. Later in the same book, the Persian Empire is seen as God's creation while Ezekiel sees the defeat of Egypt by the Babylonians as the action of the Almighty.

Written over a much shorter period, the New Testament is less specific but clearly attaches the same importance to the sovereign activity of God in human affairs. Peter proclaimed that the purpose of the Old Testament was fulfilled in Christ. Paul argued that 'there is no authority but by act of God, and the existing authorities are instituted by him'.[2] One of the most powerful of the images which Christ bequeathed to his followers was that of the Final Judgement.

The concept of redemption

It is, perhaps, the more limited notion of history as the chronicle of human redemption which comes out most immediately in the Bible and so should be discussed first. The saving activity of Almighty God is the context of Jewish convictions about racial destiny. To Christians the promise of blessing to all people through Abraham and his descendants, realized through historical developments and pressures on the people of Israel, has its climax in the advent of Jesus Christ, coming at a precise time to a precisely prepared situation. As the author of the Epistle to the Hebrews says, God spoke fragmentarily in the past but has spoken 'in this final age' by Christ; Paul says that Christ came 'in the fulness of time'. This reflects the way Jesus saw himself as the fulfiller of divine purpose whose career proceeded by God's direction to 'his hour', and who was the inaugurator of the new age and the new society, the Kingdom of God. As he said to the Jewish authorities, 'from now on the Son of Man will be seated at the right hand of Almighty God'. To Pilate he said, 'You would have no authority at all over me if it had not been granted you from above'.[3]

The Christian understanding of redemption does not, of course, end with the advent of Christ. Destiny now follows the fortunes of the Kingdom. Paul taught that the plan of God, 'to be put into effect when the time was ripe', was to bring everything 'into a unity in Christ' and in a remarkable passage in the letter to Christians at Ephesus he even asserts that the destiny of the physical creation is inextricably bound up with the new society of Christ's followers. The theme of the Revelation, significantly placed last in the New Testament canon, is the triumph of the Kingdom and the ultimate victory of a Christ who is 'King of kings and Lord of lords'. 'Alleluia! shouts a vast multitude in heaven, 'the Lord our God, sovereign over all, has entered on his reign!'[4]

Currents beneath the waves

It is, however, much easier to demonstrate Christian confidence in a divine programme of human redemption than it is to see that redemption operating in history. Very often, indeed, the events of history seem to be positively hostile to such a hypothesis. When the Romans took direct control of Judaea in AD 6 it hardly looked like the fulfilment of Jewish destiny, any more than the expulsion of Christian missionaries from China after 1949 appeared to advance the Kingdom of God.

Difficulties in the Jewish and Christian view of redemption in history have, of course, long been realized. Augustine of Hippo wrote his book *The City of God* precisely to reconcile this belief with the disastrous sack of Rome in AD 410. Strikingly, this realization is even present at the very point of its assertion in the Bible. The prophets spoke during periods of national decline which seemed to contradict absolutely the destiny of the Jewish people. The contradiction is, above all, integral in the Christian understanding of

Jesus Christ.

In human terms the life of Christ was an utter failure, a waste and a tragedy. Two of his followers are recorded as saying after the crucifixion, 'We had been hoping that he was the man to liberate Israel'. The last time his disciples saw him after the resurrection, they asked, 'Lord, is this the time when you are to establish once again the sovereignty of Israel?', and were told not to bother with questions of that kind. The experience of Christ throws up in its starkest form the apparent irrationality of the Christian claim that the salvation of man in the theme of history. But it also points the way to a resolution of the problem. In human terms a write-off, in divine terms the career of Christ was the apex of human history, the utter self-giving of the Creator in love and forgiveness. Paul called it folly; in human terms it was. But in the eyes of God it is the uttermost expression of his love. Defeat was victory, waste was glory. In other words, the hand of God in human affairs can only be understood if we can look at those human affairs from God's point of view, or to use a convenient Latin label, *sub specie aeternitatis*.[5]

The same resolution is seen when we look at the prophets. In a real sense what they were writing was not history but anti-history. Men watching from opposite sides as a tapestry is being woven will see different things, not because there are two tapestries but because the weaving of a pattern on one side will produce on the other, not a pattern but the reverse of a pattern. Because they were prophets, the prophets were bad historians. For example, thirteen verses only are devoted to the reign of Omri, king of Israel from 885/4 to 874/3 BC, although non-biblical sources indicate a highly successful ruler. What appears to the historian as effective rule is presented by the prophets as failure because the prophets were judging from God's side of the fabric.

The conclusion must be that although Christians claim that God acts specifically in history, the key to such action is not to be found in history but in an understanding of God. Not only is God, the agent, outside history, but meaning is also outside history, even though the consequences of God's actions are the events of history. Understanding belongs to the world of faith, not historical scholarship. If God acts, we cannot identify his action. Historians are like men who watch the movement of the waves under the impulse of wind and tide, but cannot see the currents.

To the critic of Christianity this may seem a cheap evasion, having one's cake and eating it. But a brief reflection will show that this is not the case. What test would we devise to identify

God's action in the world which did not require us first of all to be aware of what God intends? Since we do not have the position from which to observe, we are back with Alice on the Wonderland railway station. We are up against an insoluble problem in method.

The argument will also seem an evasion to many Christians, to those who believe, on the basis of prophetic interpretation or simple circumstance, that God's hand in history can be known. One reply would be that those who take such positions have a poor track record. It was so obvious to many eager students of prophecy before 1939 that Mussolini's Italy must be the revived Roman Empire expected on some interpretations of biblical apocalyptic. And all too often the divine purpose has been equated with 'God on our (or my) side':

> Gracious Lord, oh bomb the Germans.
>   Spare their women for Thy sake,
> And if that is not too easy
>   We will pardon Thy Mistake.
> But, gracious Lord, whate'er shall be,
> Don't let anyone bomb me.[6]

The believer, however, may respond, 'Is it not true that the Bible promises that the Jewish people will be restored to their homeland in Palestine, and have they not been restored?' Certainly this is so, but it was equally true of the Jewish people at the time of Christ; they had been exiled, and they had been restored, and they would have claimed that the biblical promises were fulfilled in their experience. The return of a Jewish state in 1948 is a fact; it is not inconsistent with a possible divine purpose, but it is certainly not proof of it. What is more, neither the return in the fifth and fourth centuries BC nor in the twentieth century AD were total restorations of the kind envisaged by the prophets. There is also the point that belief in prophecy played a part in encouraging the more recent return; it was, in some ways, a deliberate attempt to fulfil what was taken to be the meaning of the Bible.

Much the same must be said of the Christian hope of the second coming of Christ and the final triumph of God. This, in biblical terms, is the consummation of history, but by its very nature it would be a unique interruption of history and quite beyond the scholar's consideration. It is apprehended by faith and looked for with the hope of commitment. It is useless to ask the historian about 'the signs of his coming'; he does not deal with hope. He can no more say if and when a second coming will occur, than if and when there will arrive that withering away of the state promised in Marxist eschatology. We are forced back to the conclusion that God's redemptive activity in history cannot be detected by the historian, not because it may be non-existent, but because necessarily its existence is not within his field of observation.

God's 'grand design'

So far we have been considering the Bible's contention that God is engaged in a great drama of human redemption in history. What of that broader concept of divine action which we have noted is also found in the Bible: the belief in God's general control in history? It is common to suppose that this too takes the form of an over-all plan leading up to God's final triumph, indeed to see all human history as an enormous jig-saw with divine fingers putting the interlocking pieces in, one after the other, to produce a predetermined pattern. The story of redemption is the centre of that pattern, with all other events relating to it and to the final design.

Such a suggestion brings with it very serious problems. If God does work through nations as the prophets believed in the case of Israel, then the current international situation must represent his will at each given time. Was, therefore, the Russian invasion of Czechoslovakia in 1968 something which God intended, perhaps for some future purpose? Over and above this moral difficulty, it is hard to see any escape from determinism; if God wills the present and also willed the successively receding pasts, history must be a linear development. Yet what is linear development in history but chronological inevitability? Furthermore, the Christian view of history arises in a Mediterranean context. God's purposes must extend equally to the rest of the world, but the rest of the world has been quite outside the specific destiny which culminates in Christ. If there is a divine script for all history, is it not odd that only the Jews had a copy, and that only for the scenes which concerned them? In what way did, say, the substitution of the Sung Emperors in China by the Mongols fulfil the plan of God?

We can, perhaps, take some guidance at this juncture from one of those stories in history which, if not true, deserve to be. Before the Battle of Dunbar the Scots general, Leslie, had Oliver Cromwell pinned against the sea while he occupied an unassailable position on the nearby high ground. The very influential Scottish ministers urged Leslie, nevertheless, to follow Old Testament models and march down to meet this modern Canaanite; he did, and his army was routed. The temptation to project from the Bible is always hazardous, and not least the projection from the story of a divine plan of salvation to the assumption of some universal plan in history. The Old Testament prophets can mislead.

In the first place, the prophets were able to explain one element only in the history of their own day, not the totality. Voltaire observed ironically of his contemporaries who thought otherwise:

> What I admire most in our modern compilers is the wisdom and good faith with which they prove to us that everything that happened in former days in the greatest empires in the world happened only in order to instruct the inhabitants of Palestine. If the kings of Babylon in the course of their conquests fall in passing on the Hebrew people, it is solely in order to punish this people for its sins.[7]

We must assume that there are other dimensions in history other than the plan of redemption. If history means something only in relation to the final triumph of God, it will be meaningless within the compass of the seventy years or so of a man's life experience. There is no immediate significance in joining correctly two isolated pieces of a jig-saw; significance arrives hours or days later when the puzzle is complete.

In the second place, the prophetic story of the Jewish nation is unique, not typical, and not only because the prophets claimed to know what God intended, which we can never know. What the prophets say is also atypical because it is said in national terms. They portray God acting to produce a chosen nation under the pressure of surrounding nations, with the intention of arriving at a perfect community through which all mankind would be blessed, a blessing which, as we have seen, Christians believe has arrived in Christ. But this is not to say that God's purposes normally require him to act in national terms. A leading English reformer greeted the birth of the future Edward VI in 1537 with the hallelujah, 'verily he hath showed himself God of England, or rather an English God', but this identification of any other nation with the Israel of old is wholly inadmissible.[8] The Jews had a distinctive national destiny to produce the Messiah, and that was special to them. It does not entitle us to presume that there is a divine destiny for any other nation.

The new Israel

The conclusion that the national dimension of ancient Jewish prophecy is exceptional is also suggested by the New Testament view of divine purpose since the advent of Christ. The distinctive history and status of the Jews is not denied; Paul, indeed, spends a considerable time wrestling with the paradox of God's purpose for his fellow-countrymen and their rejection of the climax of that purpose, Jesus Christ. But the focus of God's purpose is now elsewhere, on the growth of the new inter-racial Christian community; as Paul wrote to Christians in Asia Minor, 'There is no question here of Greek and Jew, circumcised and uncircumcised, barbarian, Scythian, slave and freeman; but Christ is all, and is in all.'[9]

This is what the early Christians had in mind when they saw themselves as 'the new Israel'. The church (the community, of course, not the ecclesiastical machine!) is the manifestation of the new chosen people, the sons of God in every age and place, and it is with them that divine destiny principally lies. It is possible, no doubt, that nurture of the Christian community could lead God to act from time to time through large political units, but God's over-all design is no longer committed to the fortunes of one particular nation. The arena of the divine plan is no more the arena of national or international events. The spread of this Christian commonwealth is charted in individual adherence to Christ and the changing quality of that adherence.

What can the historian say of that? Is there not here, at last, something he can measure? In principle, yes, but the practical problems are severe. Spiritual progress takes place in the individual and, even more private, in the mind and emotions of that individual. This is below the level of definition which the historian can normally expect to achieve. Even the fifty and more volumes of Luther's writings tell us only part of his spiritual experience; for most men there is nothing. And no-one can know the climacteric of a Christian's life; as Charles Wesley wrote:

> Happy if with my latest breath
>   I might but gasp His name;
> Preach Him to all, and cry in death:
>   Behold, behold the Lamb![10]

It is very commonly asserted that the church is in decline in Western Europe. This may be true of organized religion, but is it true of the quality of life among believers? How can we draw up a profit and loss account for prayer, faith, character or evangelical zeal?

On occasion, of course, it is possible to suggest sources and methods which might yield something. Interpretation of the material is, however, far from simple. Does the self-analysis of a diary tell us more of the writer's psychology than of the actuality? Do the changing formulae of wills in later-medieval England indicate deeper devotion on the part of testators, new fashions in language and thought or merely that a different generation of parish priest was making the initial drafts? When a seventeenth-century gentleman took sermon notes was he necessarily concerned to respond to the call of God in that sermon? From time to time historians have been able to suggest where such pieces of evidence might seem to lead, but not over any continuous period or on a large, still less a world-wide scale. A global assessment of the growth of Christian commitment is beyond us.

Grasping the nettle

Once we grasp the nettle and recognize that there is no biblical warrant for extending the idea of God's specific blue-print for history beyond the particular national history of the Jews and, (since Christ), of the new society of his disciples, we remove many of the difficulties we have noticed. We need no longer suppose a divine initiative behind the evil in history, whether in Czechoslovakia or elsewhere. We do not have to posit some undetected divine purposes in Asia or America of assumed significance to a world-wide plan. Instead, we see God's redemptive purpose in history channelled in a brook which grows into a river and only with Christ bursts into a flood which has already made Christianity the largest religion in the world.

This way of thinking also escapes from the treadmill of determinism. It allows us to see ourselves, no less than our ancestors, as men facing real choices in history and making decisions which mean something. It removes as well the compulsion to interpret every human experience as a contribution to an overriding design. We need no longer assume that the Wall Street crash, the Second World War or the arrival of the space age have part-numbers on God's master-drawing.

The providence and sovereignty of God

To some Christians this line of argument will appear all too radical, throwing the baby out with the bathwater. To avoid problems raised by the notion of an overall divine plan, it seems that divine purpose has been abandoned for almost all human history. What is more, God's sovereignty has been undermined. But this is not the case. All that has been jettisoned is the notion of a universally applicable plan, the 'jig-saw' view of history, not the idea of divine purposes in history. Purpose and plan can be quite distinct conceptions. The confidence of biblical writers in the sovereignty of God and his interest in the world he has made is not in the least challenged.

If it is correct to conclude that we should talk only of God's plan for the progressive redemption of man, what are these other purposes behind his activity in history? The Bible everywhere asserts that God is supreme over history. God knows:

> The Lord looks out from heaven,
> he sees the whole race of men;
> he surveys from his dwelling-place
>   all the inhabitants of the earth.
> It is he who fashions the hearts of all men alike,
>   who discerns all that they do.

He is in control: 'Kingly power belongs to the Lord, and dominion over the nations is his'. He acts in history: 'He deposes kings and sets them up'. And the purpose of this supremacy is clear; its one end is the vindication of morality.

> [The Lord's] eye is upon mankind,
> he takes their measure at a glance.
> The Lord weighs just and unjust
>   and hates with all his soul the lover of violence.[11]

The principle that morality regulates history is as firmly rooted in Old Testament thought as the more prominent notion of a special destiny for the Jewish nation. Often, indeed, the themes intertwine, with immorality being punished at one level and historical destiny being advanced at another. Sometimes, indeed, moral consequence is seen to operate in such a way as to advance the progress of that destiny. It is the importance of morality in human affairs which also informs much of the prophetic comment on non-Jewish people. It is taken as axiomatic that there is a direct divine sanction against evil.

> Tyrants lose their strength and are brought low
>   in the grip of misfortune and sorrow;
> he brings princes into contempt
>   and leaves them wandering in a trackless waste.
> But the poor man he lifts clear of his troubles
>   and makes families increase like flocks of sheep.

There is also an ultimate sanction in the day of judgement:

The Lord thunders, he sits enthroned for ever:
  he has set up his throne, his judgement-seat.
He it is who will judge the world with justice
  and try the cause of the peoples fairly.

For soon the day of the Lord will come on all nations:
  you shall be treated as you have treated others,
  and your deeds will recoil on your own head.

As the Bible understands it, overall purpose in history is concerned with morality.[12]

It is even possible to argue that in terms of what the Bible teaches about the created world, this general moral purpose is original to existence in a way that the redemptive design in history is not. In the creation narrative in Genesis we are told of a moral dimension to the universe; 'God saw all that he had made, and it was very good'. Man was created in a moral relationship to God, to love him and obey him. Man's connection with the rest of creation was a moral one also; he was to 'be fruitful and increase, fill the earth and subdue it, rule over...every living thing'.[13]

The need for the divine plan of redemption follows from the disregard of the morality inherent in the creation. Its object is to cancel man's moral bankruptcy and to restore his moral capital. Its achievement will be the recovery of a moral perfection for the whole creation, what Peter called 'new heavens and a new earth, the home of justice'.[14] Without the moral dimension inherent, as the Bible sees it, in the essential nature of the creation, the notion that man needs to be redeemed by God makes no sense at all. To argue that divine purpose in history should be seen as the operation of morality is, therefore, to stand on the fundamental nature of what the Bible understands existence to be.

When we recognize that the divine plan in history is for the redemption of men in Chirst, we do not thereby abandon belief in either the sovereignty of God or his involvement in the world. This specific continuous plan in history is unique. The Bible insists that it is God's moral activity which is the atmosphere in which all men live and all history takes place. And to this claim we must now turn.

Notes and references
1 Robert Bolton, *Hypocritica* (*c* 1618), quoted in *The Evolution of British Historiography*, ed. J.R.Hale, Macmillan, 1967, p. 12.

2 Romans 13:1.

3 Hebrews 1:2, Galatians 4:4, Ephesians 1:10; Luke 22:69; John 19:11.

4 Ephesians 1:10; Revelation 17:14, 19:6.

5 Luke 24:21; Acts 1:6.

6 John Betjeman, *Collected Poems*, J.Murray, 1958, p. 84.

7 Voltaire, *The Age of Louis XIV and other selected writings*, ed. J.H.Brumfitt, Dent, 1966, p. 320.

8 Hugh Latimer to Thomas Cromwell, *Literary Remains of Edward VI*, ed. J.G.Nichols, Roxburghe Club 1857, p. xxiii.

9 Colossians 3:11.

10 Charles Wesley, 'Jesus! the name high over all'.

11 Psalm 33:13–15; 22:28; Daniel 2:21; Psalm 11:4–5.

12 Psalm 107:39–41; 9:7–8; Obadiah:15.

13 Genesis 1:31; 1:28.

14 2 Peter 3:13.

Chapter 7

Destiny and morality: a world of consequences?

Among the maxims attributed to Napoleon Bonaparte is, 'God is on the side of the big battalions.' In fact the saying is at least as old as Louis XIV's general, Turenne, and for good reason. It seems to sum up the evidence of history: virtue is irrelevant, what counts is power.

The indigenous people of Estonia and Livonia were subjugated by thirteenth-century German crusaders, divided in the sixteenth century between Swedes and Poles, in the next held by Sweden alone and in the eighteenth captured by Russia which has controlled them ever since, except for two decades of freedom between 1918 and 1939 – the only time in seven hundred years in which they controlled their own fortunes. The moral qualities of the contending parties never mattered. What counted was the current balance of force. A world empire was not the reward of British virtue any more than its loss has been the consequence of British depravity. Innocence did not protect the Jews from Nazi extermination.

The paradox of justice

Faced with evidence of this kind, the Christian belief that morality operates in history appears simply untrue. And yet, as we have seen, it is not an optional extra to the faith; it arises from belief in a God who is supreme and who is good. Paul preached that God is 'the universal giver of life and breath and all else'; he wrote that God is 'Source, Guide and Goal of all that is.'[1] If, therefore, morality does not operate in human affairs, either God is not good or belief in his power is mistaken. This is the dilemma which underlies the common reaction to tragedy or evil, 'Why does God allow this?' As a prominent journalist and former war-correspondent once said, 'When you have seen as much horror and death as I have, you can't believe in a God.'

What makes the problem more poignant is that the vision of a morally ordered world is one of the great human dreams. The Old

Testament writers who make the most of this theme are far beyond the primitive tribal outlook that 'good' meant advantageous to the Jews and 'bad' the opposite. The prophet Amos, for example, surveyed the international scene of the mid-eighth century BC and announced judgement on nation after nation for its crimes: the Aramean kingdom of Damascus for brutality, the city states of Gaza and Tyre and the kingdom of Edom for slave-trading, the Ammonites for territorial expansionism, the Moabites for atrocities, the Jews of Jerusalem for idolatry, the Israelites of Samaria for social injustice. His contemporary, Isaiah, prophesied doom to Assyria because of its arrogant militarism: 'his thought is only to destroy and to wipe out nation after nation.'[2] The Babylonian state, too, was to fall and suffer the wholesale, insensitive exploitation it had meted out to others. Here we have, if not history as it is, then history as it ought to be.

The difficulty in relating the vision of a moral world to the apparent reality was, of course, well known to the prophets themselves. It is often said that the book of Job is concerned with the problem of suffering. In fact it is concerned with the problem of morality – how can God be righteous when the good suffer? The answer it gives is, however, not a direct one. Instead it points to the infinity of God and the finite character of man; in other words there is no problem when looked at from God's point of view, i.e. *sub specie aeternitatis*.

Psalm 73 gives a specific account of a prophet reaching this same conclusion. He sees that the wicked flourish, that God seems blind, that righteous living appears a waste of time, and he realizes that to think in this way will destroy his belief.

> So I set myself to think this out
> but I found it too hard for me,
> until I went into God's sacred courts;
>   there I saw clearly what their end would be.[3]

The search for judgement in human affairs finds its end in the recognition of the sovereignty of God. The outcome of this recognition is prophetic activity. Given that God is supreme, the prophet does not ask 'Is God's judgement seen in history?' but 'What is God judging in history at this moment?' The judgements of God are perceived when a confidence that they exist reacts with an awareness of contemporary events.

A good example of this is the Old Testament contrast between the 'false' and the 'true' prophet. The false prophet saw only in the short-term; for him immediate prosperity for Israel, made possible when the attention of the great powers was diverted elsewhere, was a sure indication of divine approval. The true prophet recognized the deep moral decadence of the nation and interpreted the impending national collapse as divine punishment. Morality was to be experienced in suffering, and through suffering and repentence was to come restoration. The experience of exile in Babylon and the return to Palestine were, therefore, both held to demonstrate morality in action.

In exactly the same way, the faith that Jesus had in the morality of the universe made him willing to accept the risk of crucifixion against all the advice of his friends. Indeed, confidence in the morality, the 'righteousness' of God, underlay what Christ saw as the significance of his own death, that it was 'for others'. By accepting in himself the literal consequences of human evil, the way would be opened for men to enter into Christ's new life. As the First Letter of Peter says:

> When he suffered he uttered no threats, but committed his cause to the One who judges justly. In his own person he carried our sins to the gibbet, so that we might cease to live for sin and begin to live for righteousness. By his wounds you have been healed.[4]

From this prophetic vision the historian must stand aside. Just as a divine plan in human events is not perceptible to historical enquiry, neither is the significance which the prophet sees in this event or that. The believer who asks the historian, 'Don't you think that God is judging...?' can only receive the answer 'Not from my point of view.' It is possible to analyse a picture in scientific terms – as paint; it is also possible to analyse the same picture in artistic terms – as a painting. According to the way we organize knowledge today, the two descriptions will be complementary but separate; each will be completely valid and each will be distinct from the other. Likewise, history and prophecy are fully autonomous.

Morality in human affairs

The problem with the *sub specie aeternitatis* argument is that it can easily seem like producing a rabbit out of the hat, or more literally, a *deus ex machina*; it evades historical criticism by occupying a historically unassailable position. The biblical critic, too, may feel that it does less than justice to the Old Testament. The Jewish prophets resolved their problem of morality in an apparently immoral world by taking the problem out of history and giving it a religious answer, but there is more than this in the way the Bible understands righteousness in human affairs. This is not that a particular right or wrong act necessarily brings a particular judgement, but that morality, as we saw in the last chapter, is the divine principle in history. Indeed, the Bible is explicit that every event does *not* have an immediate moral significance. When Christ was told of certain recent disasters, he said of the victims: 'Do you imagine they were more guilty than all the other people living in Jerusalem? I tell you they were not, but unless you repent, you will all of you come to the same end.'[5]

We will be misled if we look only at specific acts of morality and immorality and conclude that God understands the justice involved, even if we do not, and that all will be revealed to the prophetically insensitive among us in the life to come. We need to face the assertion of Amos, Isaiah, the other prophets and the Bible as a whole that morality operates in the world in general. No doubt this, too, is more intelligible in the light of heaven, but the Christian asks a lot of the historian if he expects him to accept the existence of a universally operative principle in human affairs which is entirely undetectable: *sub specie aeternitatis* is not the answer here.

This more general view of morality in history is even more important because, once again, it goes back to the heart of what Christians believe about God. The Bible sees the grace of God, his loving, outgoing activity, as the universal medium in which mankind exists. The murderer wields the knife with a strength and dexterity that God gives; the artist creates or performs with a skill that comes from God; the lifeboatmen who set out in the storm go in the power of God. And if this is the case, then all history must be judgement – on the misuse of that knife, on the quality of that art, on the degree of that dedication.

The Christian, however, does not hold a doctrine of inevitable *karma*. God's grace is also a positive factor in all circumstances. God is incessantly acting in his world for good. Jesus said that God 'makes his sun to rise on good and bad alike, and sends the rain on the honest and the dishonest'. In the world of men this grace is just as active, so that Isaiah could refer to the tolerant but pagan emperor of Persia as God's 'anointed whom he has taken by the hand'. Indeed, without the initiative of God in history, what Christians call the action of the Holy Spirit, the biblical concept of a divine plan to redeem man is unintelligible. The whole basis of Christianity is that the world is a world of consequences but it is also a world where the law of consequence is influenced and can be interrupted by divine love.[6]

The search for morality in history brings us, therefore, face to face both with the problem of grace and with the problem of judgement.

The grace of God

If history is the record of God's grace in action, there is no disguising the fact that the record appears damning. Edmund Blunden wrote a *Report on Experience:*

I have been young, and now am not too old;
And I have seen the righteous forsaken,
His health, his honour and his quality taken.
   This is not what we were formerly told.

I have seen a green country, useful to the race,
Knocked silly with guns and mines, its villages vanished,
Even the last rat and last kestrel banished —
   God bless us all, this was peculiar grace.

I knew Seraphina, Nature gave her hue,
Glance, sympathy, note, like one from Eden.
I saw her smile warp, heard her lyric deaden;
   She turned to harlotry — this I took to be new.

Say what you will, our God sees how they run.
These disillusions are His curious proving
That he loves humanity and will go on loving;
   Over them are faith, life, virtue in the sun.

This complaint is, of course, not the same as the question: 'Why does suffering exist?' That is clearly cognate with the issue of morality in history, but it is also distinct. History is not concerned with the meaning of existence. Its brief, in Ranke's words, is to deal with events 'as they actually happened' and it finds no difficulty in accepting pain and evil as part of the way 'things are'. The challenge here is that immorality in history does not seem to be met by the positive counter of God's grace. His 'curious' way of 'proving that he loves humanity' is to let the big battalions win.[7]

To reach this conclusion is very easy, but two comments may be made. First, the ability of men to resist the grace of God is no comment on that grace itself. It is the price to be paid if man is to have a free moral choice. Herbert Butterfield wrote:

When we think of the action of God in history we need not imagine a heavy hand interposed to interfere with the workings of a heavy piece of machinery. Perhaps a better picture of our situation would be that of a child who played her piece very badly when she was alone, but when the music-teacher sat at her side played it passably well, though the music-teacher never touched her, never said anything, but operated by pure sympathetic attraction and by just being there.[8]

But no-one who has been taught music or seen a child taught music will doubt the ease with which the teacher's influence can be countered by obstinacy or lack of interest. 'You cannot make them practise!' The grace of God guarantees our privilege to reject it.

In the second place, it must be the case that the positive actions of God are, for the reasons previously considered, demonstrable only to faith. The possibility that he acts must always be there because, in Butterfield's words, 'there is no such self-contained intellectual system as would forbid a man who was a historian to believe that God Himself is a factor in history.'[9] Yet no historian *as historian* can ever claim to have established that God does act and what his specific actions have been.

There are, of course, instances where the Christian historian may see what he feels can only be described as 'God-shaped blanks' in history. He may note the *charisma* of a Martin Luther or an Ignatius Loyola and the timely arrival of a Pope John XXIII, provided that he also recognizes the possibility of perverted grace in the magnetism of an Adolf Hitler. He may suggest, with Elie Halévy, that the Methodist revival saved Britain from the Jacobins at the time of the French Revolution, provided that he also faces up to the criticism of E.P.Thompson that Methodism 'mediated the work-discipline of industrialism' and was also 'in some part a reflex of despair among the working population'.[10]

As he examines the record of the past, the Christian is bound to ponder on the possible evidence of God's grace. For example, Herbert Butterfield suggested that as we look back on certain episodes such as the Fire of London in 1666, the wars between Catholic and Protestant in the sixteenth and seventeenth centuries, the American Revolution, we can see a beneficial outcome where, at the time, there was only tragedy. This is very near to the verse from the Psalms which, in the Authorized Version, reads 'the wrath of man shall praise Thee'. He pointed further to the fact that 'millions of men ... conscious of nothing save going about their own business, have together woven a fabric better in many respects than any of them knew'. God is not 'progress', nor is 'progress' the universal law in history, but even an atheist may marvel at the sheer capacity of the spirit of man to survive and triumph. And what of the 'tide' of history, the momentum of events and actions which make puny the efforts of statesmen and the greatest of power systems? Was Bismarck justified when he said that 'the statesman must try and reach for the hem when he hears the garment of God rustling through events' or is the tide in the affairs of men random and accidental?[11]

Yet although the Christian may see what he takes to be evidence of grace, he is not, at this point, entitled to leap up and acclaim the Almighty. Perceptions of this kind belong to the world of faith. If he is to be honest to the canons of his subject he must not add 'God' to the recognized cast list of history. But when he reflects privately on the grace of God in human experience he is not indulging an irrational private delusion. What the Marxist sees as the working of the dialectical process in history – thesis meeting antithesis and resulting in a new synthesis, or what A.J.Toynbee saw as a process of environmental challenge and human response may be equally intelligible in terms of providence. Or these mechanisms, if they exist, could themselves be exhibitions of the working of providence.

The student of history has to realize that in setting out to be a historian he is accepting a convention which limits his analysis. In the last two hundred years the assumption that different branches of knowledge must be treated as autonomous has been an essential factor in enabling man to maximize his knowledge. Yet it is a convenience of analysis, not a response to truth – far from it. The Mona Lisa is paint on canvas; it is also a painting. We take an intact experience and compartmentalize it so that we can understand it better, but it remains a whole. To quote Butterfield again:

> Those who say that everything in history can be explained without bringing God into the argument would be doing no more than walking round in a circle, even if it were true that anything in history had yet been fully explained. A world of blind men might equally maintain that their universe was explicable to them without the introduction of a foreign concept like the notion of light.[12]

The student of history puts on, if not dark glasses, at least glasses which filter out all non-natural wavelengths, but he is gullible if he imagines that he can see everything that can be. Over us could be 'faith, life, virtue in the sun'.

Judgement in history

In grappling with the second part of the challenge – the need to show God's judgement in history – we have to clear away a number of distractions. First we must rid ourselves of crude assumptions about what judgement in history might be, the sort of error which the false prophets of the Old Testament fell into. The Bible gives us no reason to imagine that morality in history reveals itself in the fashion of a divine 'stick and carrot'. History, indeed, is full of examples of those who have deserved the one but received the other. Jesuit schools in France for English Catholics used to perform a play of the Reformation which had Henry VIII tormented by devils, a fate which the audience devoutly believed had now befallen Henry, but which the king had inconveniently avoided while alive. The frequently heard assertion among certain groups of preacher that Victorian prosperity was the result of Victorian piety and that Britain's post-war difficulties have been the consequence of twentieth century agnosticism, shows an ignorance of both economics and religion.

The Henry VIII example is, furthermore, an illustration of another error, that of seeing judgement in history as judgement upon individuals. To ask the question 'Who died in his bed, full of years and honour?' is to enter the realm of personal ethics, not history. Morality in history, if it exists as the Bible claims, must act at the level of the community, not the individual. It is also important not to be hasty. Judgement in biblical terms is rarely immediate, it is upon 'the third and fourth generation'. Indeed, perhaps the most challenging element in Old Testament morality is the idea that the consequences of wrong doing extend beyond the immediate wrong-doer.

Earthquakes and Acts of God excepted

We also need to ask ourselves some fundamental questions about the nature of morality in human affairs. Here our attitudes and beliefs are often naive in the extreme. As we have seen, the Christian approach to science has long ago abandoned the notion of God coolly upsetting normal procedures by arbitrary behaviour. We now see nature as a fluid network of relationships with the action of God pervading the whole. Laws in nature are not eternal absolutes but ways in which the world has been observed to behave.

Our approach to the possibility of divine involvement in human affairs is, however, still at the arbitrary interference stage. Christians cling to a catastrophe theology, acquiescing in the legal notion of an act of God, that is, something which occurs by pure chance. So they ask 'Why should this have happened to…?' when all the time Christ has given them the answer, 'Unless you repent, you will all come to the same end.' In other words, the principle that wrong is punished is generally operative, not occasionally invoked. The moral judgement of God in history is not to be sought in specific punishments which must have resulted from specific wrongs but in broad and long-term consequences.

If a man walks over a cliff, he will probably be killed, not because God has specially created gravity to punish him for his evil living, but because gravity is one of the fundamental relationships in the natural world, upon which existence depends. He has ignored this and he takes the consequences. In the same way it is possible to think of moral principles as fundamental to human existence. Dietrich Bonhoeffer wrote that 'the world *is* simply ordered in such a way that a profound respect for the absolute laws and human rights is also the best means of self-preservation'.[13] Defiance of these principles brings retribution to generations yet unborn and to individuals entirely innocent of the initial wrong. Perhaps, indeed, God's action should be seen as a uniform continuum. His upholding of nature appears to differ from his righteous judgement in human societies only because the means of observation possessed by the scientist and by the historian are different.

The possibility that moral law is cognate with scientific law may, at first sight, appear to put God's sovereignty in a mechanistic straight-jacket Such a suggestion, however, would be false, on two grounds. As we have seen, law in this context is an observed regularity in the way the world operates, or in Christian terms, the way we observe God to work. Law does not exist apart from God; it is not a limitation on his independence; it is the way he acts and expresses his will. Secondly, to say that actions are regular does not mean that they are routine. The vision of Jesus was of a God who 'never overlooks a sparrow'.[14] If Jesus was right, then every operation of law, scientific or moral, is also God's specific will. His will may be to act regularly, but every regular act is his particular will.

Judgement at work

If we are correct to conclude that judgement operates in history as a kind of law, a second question we have to ask is 'What do we understand divine retribution in human society to be?' The helpful analogy here comes not from science but from private ethics. Individual wrong-doing only rarely receives direct punishment. Human penal institutions often deal with what Christianity sees as lesser crimes, and by no means all of these. Are the rest un-punished? By no means, the penalty is inherent in the sin. The penalty for selfishness is being a selfish person; the punishment for materialism is to drown in possessions; the reward of lechery is the coarsening of sexual response.

If we apply this insight to society in general, we will find that we have a historical truism: a society has to bear the consequences of its own actions. And not only its own actions; history shows that in many ways the human race is a unity, and the behaviour of one community can result in disaster for another totally uninvolved. In other words, God's judgement on mankind is for mankind to create the world it lives in. As the Old Testament prophet Hosea proclaimed: 'You have ploughed wickedness into your soil, and the crop is mischief; you have eaten the fruit of treachery.'[15]

We have had a great deal of theory. How would this analysis apply in practice? No citizen of either the United States of America or of Britain today is 'to blame' for the slave trade, but the racial problem of each society is the actual historical consequence of that inhumanity. The sins of the fathers are literally being visited on the children. The traumas and consequences of decolonization can similarly be seen as judgement on the initial exploitation. So too, as Herbert Butterfield argued most powerfully, the holocaust of the Third Reich was the penalty for Prussian militarism. In con-temporary politics we are aware of the greed of the West in con-suming an excessive proportion of the raw materials available, and can prophesy a punitive reaction by the Third World. Equally, an ecological backlash will punish an inability to control human reproduction and a nuclear holocaust threatens to be the ultimate punishment of the arms-race. None of these depends upon a specifically Christian or even religious appraisal; they represent the evident conclusions and probabilities of history.

Of course the argument that morality operates in history in the form of the consequences of human action does not imply a fixed law of retribution. The evil done by a community passes into the bloodstream of the human community and mixes with many other particles to produce an effect often remote from the source of in-fection. In 1655 the frightful slaughter of the Piedmontese Protestants by the Duke of Savoy, under French encouragement, drew from Milton the famous sonnet, 'On the Late Massacre in Piedmont':

Avenge, O Lord, thy slaughter'd saints, whose bones
  Lie scatter'd on the Alpine mountains cold.

Milton believed that sin brought its own punishment and he visualized retribution coming in a new generation which would throw off the tyranny of the Roman Catholic church; instead it came in the form of the Inquisition which deadened Piedmontese society for generations. Equally, punishment does not always strike where we would expect. American military hubris perhaps met its judgement in Vietnam, but Russia's *Gulag Archipelago* remains unavenged. But if human society is like the natural world, a network of relationships and responses, the observer asks when and how judgement will come, not whether it will come. The action has occurred, the reaction is in train.

The context, of course, is always the context of God's grace and the time-scale is the time-scale of macro-history. Jesus once asked: 'Will not God vindicate his chosen who cry out to him day and night, while he delays to help them? I tell you he will vindicate them soon enough.'[16] Immediate, finite perspectives will reveal nothing, but over the years morality does work its judgements. Can anyone in Great Britain and Ireland in this last quarter of the twentieth century doubt that tolerating injustice and fostering communal hatred has brought retribution in the gun and the bomb?

To believe that judgement operates in history is to accept that human affairs are the consequence of human actions. It is not the historical equivalent of believing in the Phlogiston Principle, that illusory factor in combustion whose presence was assumed but could never be demonstrated. It is, rather, to stand on the nature of history itself.

Notes and references

1 Acts 17:25; Romans 11:36.

2 Isaiah 10:5, 7.

3 Psalm 73:16–17.

4 1 Peter 2:23–24.

5 Luke 13:4–5.

6 Matthew 5:45; Isaiah 45:1.

7 *The Penguin Book of English Verse*, ed. J.Hayward (1956), pp. 450–51; Leopold Ranke, *History of the Romano-German People* (1825), extracts in F.Stern, *The Varieties of History*, Macmillan, 2nd edn. 1970, p. 57.

8 H.Butterfield, *Christianity and History*, G.Bell, 1954, p. 111.

9 *Ibid.* p. 108.

10 E.P.Thompson, *The Making of the English Working Classes*, Penguin Books, 1968, p. 441.

11 Psalm 76:10; Butterfield, *Christianity and History* pp. 96, 100.
12 *Ibid.* p. 107.
13 Dietrich Bonhoeffer, *Letters and Papers from Prison,* ed. E.Bethge, Collins, 1959, p. 141–2.
14 Luke 12:6.
15 Hosea 10:13.
16 Luke 18:7–8.

Chapter 8

The historical perspective

'God defend me from my friends; from my enemies I can defend myself'! So runs the old proverb. Readers of this book may feel something like this if they already have a Christian commitment. I have said all the wrong things. To some this will have appeared a betrayal of the cause and a missed opportunity to spell out with confidence and vigour the truth which Christians believe. To others it will have appeared an unfortunate attempt to resurrect an out-of-date Christianity of creeds and dogmas; the day for this is over, discipleship – following Christ – is what counts. And between the two stands the onlooker. Who is right, the dogmatist or the disciple? We have seen something of the historical basis for Christianity and the philosophy of history which it derives from the Bible. What is the relationship between this historical dimension and the active faith of the Christian today?

A betrayal
It is entirely understandable to react with hostility to the clinical appraisal of any cherished belief. 'Why does he not come out firmly with the truth – the historic, risen, divine Jesus is the lord and righteous judge of history?' Instead, the fact of the resurrection has been qualified, the action of God in the world has been blurred and the authoritative scriptural view of history has been impugned. To echo a sixteenth-century comment, 'the lukewarm do not go to Paradise, even if they are called moderates.'[1]

This reaction is, nevertheless, unwarranted. It misunderstands the weight which the Christian can put on the support of history, indeed, on rational argument of any kind. Christian writers can hope to show that the faith does not offend reason, is not incompatible with the best modern understanding of the world, is not impractical in what it requires. But what they cannot do is to prove that the faith is true. And they are wrong if they try.

It is false to Jesus himself to set out to establish Christianity as an irrefutable, objective system. His challenge was always restrained; he never swept people away by the force of his personality. It was essential in asking for voluntary commitment to leave men the option to reject him. What is more, he called men to follow him, not merely to accept that what he said was correct. Indeed, for Jesus the only possible responses were action and inaction, not belief and unbelief. To believe was to act, not to act was not to believe.

This remains true. If it were possible to prove the resurrection of Christ in every detail, what would that mean? Supposing a man did rise from the dead in April AD 30 or 33; this carries no compulsion for men and women today. Precedent and custom may be dear to the hearts of men, but the past can never force a particular response from the present, any more than the present can bind the future. If the return of Christ from the dead could be established on the same terms as Neville Chamberlain's return from Munich in 1938, there is nothing to stop the reaction: 'So what?' To be a Christian is a matter of response, not factual conviction, as Jesus well knew: 'If they do not listen to Moses and the prophets, they will pay no heed even if someone should rise from the dead.'[2] It does no good to bludgeon people with the historical case for Christianity, firm though the previous chapters have argued this to be. The response to Christ is not to a figure in history, but to the 'man for today', the living Lord who here and now seeks the allegiance of every human personality.

Outworn creeds

At this point the protagonists of discipleship will sigh with relief. At long last we have reached something remotely up-to-date. There are fashions in ideas as well as fashions in dress, and it cannot be denied that the argument of the previous chapters has been unfashionable to a degree. Discussion has been in the form of propositions – that there are truths which can be confirmed or refuted by rational analysis. The resurrection of Christ has been examined as an alleged event in history; the activity and justice of God have been looked for in the actual fabric of history. But in theological circles in this century, propositional truths have been unpopular. As *Christian Believing*, the 1976 report of the Doctrine Commission of the Church of England, remarked, one important contemporary attitude to belief is that 'the essence of faith is to be found in a life of discipleship rather than in credal affirmations'.[3]

This emphasis, that it is life and living which really matter, is a response to important developments in European thought over the last century and most noticeably to the ideas which originate in the work of the Danish philosopher and religious thinker, Sören Kierkegaard (1813–55). It is to Kierkegaard that we trace the sources of modern existentialism in both its Christian and its secular forms. And much profound twentieth century theology, especially in the Germanic tradition, has been existentialist in character.

Truth for me

The conviction of Kierkegaard and those who have followed him is that what matters in a man is the quality of the response he makes to the fundamental demands of existence. With many people the response is trivial and thoughtless, and all they have is 'life'. Serious, deliberate, committed response, on the other hand, authenticates the 'existence' of the individual who makes the commitment. Many readers would find the terms easier to understand if instead of 'life' and 'existence' we had the contrast of 'mere existence' and 'real living', but Kierkegaard never set out to make his views easy. Secular and Christian existentialists part company over the nature of this committed response, since to the Christian the object of commitment is God, but they share the emphasis on action. As Kierkegaard said, 'The highest is not to understand the highest, but to do it.'

The result of such an emphasis must be a reversal of what we normally take religion to be: belief only has significance if it is expressed in terms of individual human will and decision. Much of this thinking, indeed, has been a response to the problem of living a Christian life in the twentieth century world and to the question which constantly faces the Christian minister, 'How is Christianity relevant to men today?' Kierkegaard's original approach was a deliberate reaction against speculative theology and conventional church-going alike. The only truth that matters is subjective, 'truth-for-me'. An abstract conviction that all men are equal before God only has meaning as I embrace someone of another colour as my brother.

This is, without doubt, a fundamental Christian insight and it represents a recovery of a crucial and authentic element in New Testament belief. There 'life' is contrasted with 'death' much as existentialists contrast 'authentic' with 'unauthentic' existence; we find the antithesis of 'life in the Spirit' and 'life in the flesh', and concepts such as 'the new birth'. The very sacrament of baptism was, to the early church, a symbol of burial and resurrection. To recover this is to perform for the church in the twentieth century a salutary service of the utmost importance. Christianity is nothing if it is not 'an adventure, a voyage of discovery, a journey sustained by faith and hope, towards a final and complete communion with Love at the heart of all things'.[4] The gospel calls me to faith.

On the other hand, the fact remains that many who argue most strongly for Christianity as discipleship first and foremost, do so as an alternative to the propositional element in the faith. Again to quote *Christian Believing*:

> For such Christians both doctrines and dogmas are so inadequate to the living Reality of whom they are the theological formulations that they cannot command full commitment or loyalty.

And it is more than the inadequacy of existing propositions; it is the impossibility of a propositional approach. As the chairman of the Doctrine Commission wrote in a personal statement:

> If the definition of belief were central to Christian faith that would be a profoundly worrying phenomenon. But faith is not just intellectual assent to a series of belief statements about God and Jesus. It is a response of the whole person to the ultimate reality of the world as apprehended through Jesus and the tradition springing from him.[5]

This scepticism may be arrived at from a number of starting points. Kierkegaard founded his assessment of Christianity on the unbridgeable gulf that must exist between a finite, sinful man and God 'the absolutely Unknown'. Searching for the historic evidence for Christianity was, therefore, a dangerous irrelevance, dangerous because an alternative to the only possible existential reaction to that gulf, faith. No man can reason himself into a relationship with God, still less guarantee that God will accept him; he is forced to make a gesture of total faith, a leap of despair.

The very notion of 'God in Christ' is a paradox; it can only be accepted by a faith which sacrifices our cherished pretensions to rationality. It is as if a man discovers himself in the room of a burning building. The smoke prevents his seeing how high he is from the ground and whether there is a sheet to catch him or a row of spikes: he only knows that if he stays he will burn, and from a situation so impossible he jumps in faith.

God, the ground of being

Another prominent scholar who is distrustful of propositions is Paul Tillich (1886–1965). He too starts from the position that God is totally other than man, but claims that he is the 'ground of being' or, rather, puts the point the opposite way, 'the name of this infinite and inexhaustible ground of history is *God*.'[6] What, therefore, is mystical experience? The answer is that certain events evoke ecstasy and this is an 'original' revelation of the reality of this depth of being; it is also possible to react later to the original 'sign-event', and this is a 'dependent' revelation.

The Christ event was one such original revelation. The first disciples expected Jesus to be the inaugurator of a new age. When this hope collapsed in the blood of Good Friday, it was replaced by the recognition that Jesus was, instead, the 'new being', the person who has made the complete act of existential commitment. Since the original revelation, the church has experienced continuous revelation dependent on the initial sign-event as fresh individuals have come up against Christ. Clearly Tillich's view implies a real crucifixion and also a real experience by the disciples subsequent to that death which allowed them to apply to Jesus the symbolic designation 'risen from dead'. What was that experience? The best suggestion is an ecstatic explosion produced by the tension between knowing Jesus was dead and being convinced that it was impossible for the new being to be snuffed out, but this, Tillich insists, is only conjecture.

'Demythologizing' Christianity

The most immediate influence undermining propositional religion is that of Rudolf Bultmann (1884–1976). Unlike Kierkegaard and Tillich, Bultmann began work as a historical student of the biblical text and became known as one of the severest 'form critics' of the Synoptic Gospels. His conclusion, in effect, was that these Gospels were late in date but that in them certain original sayings and deeds of Christ can be discerned. This did not directly cut across Christian belief since it is clear that what we know of apostolic preaching, the *kerygma*, is older than those Gospels. But it did reinforce the notion that we can know Christ only as preached by his followers. As an earlier scholar, Martin Kähler (1835–1912), had argued, the Christ of history is the post-resurrection Christ, not the Christ of the years before the cross; 'the real Christ is the preached Christ.'[7]

For Bultmann, therefore, the prime need is to discover how the significance of the *kerygma* can be expressed for today. There are, he says, two faces of the Christian message. One is its permanent significance, for all men in all ages; the other is the particular trappings of first-century language and ideas in which it happens to be expressed by the New Testament. These formations are totally outmoded today and have the effect of driving men away from attention to the eternal meaning of the *kerygma*. In technical terms, the trappings are 'myth', the language in which abstract truth is often expressed by ancient or non-Westernized societies. To penetrate through the myth to the reality is to 'demythologize', Bultmann's most frequently discussed idea; it is to expose the truth which the myth preserves. For example, the preaching of the Christian hope of the resurrection

> means that the man who trusts in the grace of God, and who lets go all anxiety about security, is also freed from all fear of death. He knows that he is not the one who has to worry about his future. God takes care of it; God has given him his future and therefore God's grace encounters him even in death. We cannot, of course, form any clear picture of a life after death. Yet it belongs to the radical surrender to God's grace that we renounce all pictures of a future after death and hand over everything to the grace of God, who gives us what is to come. God is always the God who comes.[8]

The fact of Jesus is 'an historical event wrought out in time and place', but its significance is across history. His divine origin, virgin birth, miracles, resurrection, ascension and second coming which we find proclaimed in the New Testament, are 'myths' which express that significance.

When we come to the creeds of the Christian church we have to be even more careful. These put the 'myths' of the New Testament into the propositional categories of Greek philosophy and, Bultman tells us, complete the alienation of the thinking modern man from Christ. The point was well put by an Anglican scholar, A.E.Harvey, during the discussion arising from *Christian Believing*:

> The biblical revelation made its way in the Western world at the cost of being drastically translated into the terms and concepts of a highly abstract and propositional philosophical tradition.
>
> Such was the enduring power of this metaphysical framework, and so brilliant were some of the thinkers who carried out the original work of translation and adaptation, that from very early times Christianity has established itself as a logically coherent system of propositional doctrines. This pre-eminence of doctrinal formulation has now been challenged both by philosophical schools in the West which are critical of any metaphysical construction, and by new expressions of Christian belief in other parts of the world where the Western philosophical tradition is essentially alien.[9]

Commitment to what?

With critics abroad of the power of Kierkegaard, Tillich and Bultmann and others scarcely less formidable, the attempt of this book
to express the Christian faith in propositional terms may appear
immodest and foolhardy. Is it not better to accept that it is commitment which matters, not credal statement? As the opening of
this chapter has argued, commitment is unquestionably the
critical test of Christian faith. Without commitment in and
through ordinary living, there is nothing, mere words. 'I believe in
God' must be a different order of statement from 'I believe in
William the Conqueror'; in the words of Jesus: 'Not everyone who
calls me "Lord, Lord" will enter the kingdom of Heaven, but only
those who do the will of my heavenly Father.' But is it possible to call
for commitment without asking 'commitment to what or to whom'?
If we accept that we can say almost nothing about the historical Jesus,
it is hard to see what is left for faith. To quote Professor R.P.C.Han-
son from another context:

> The doctrine is so much attenuated that the reader may be par-
> doned if he concludes that, whether the doctrine be true or not,
> it is not worth believing: no resurrection; no incarnation; no
> divinity of Christ. Such a doctrine, to use a forcible phrase of
> Professor A.A.Lucas, would not convert a hen.[10]

Christianity calls for response as Kierkegaard says, but the en-
titlement to make that call rests ultimately upon the meaning of
the actual event of Jesus. Without the meaning, the event is
meaningless, but without the event, there can be no meaning.
History gives the actuality, faith proclaims the significance. In the
fable of the 'Emperor's New Clothes', it took a child to cry out
that the ruler's much admired new attire was his birthday suit, and
to a non-specialist, some modern sophisticated theology seems to
leave the believer naked of all religion. We may agree that
Christianity does express some of the 'great commonplaces' of
living, but if it only does this it is no saving faith, still less a faith
grounded in history. Christianity is reduced to fable, and takes its
place alongside *Androcles and the Lion* or the story of Narcissus.

A second difficulty with the anti-propositional approach to
Christianity is its complexity. How does it answer the simple question, 'Is Christianity true?' It is no good replying that such a crude
question is meaningless; it is what ordinary men and women do
ask. To reply with a philosophical analysis of both the question
and the terms used will probably be unintelligible to the ordinary
practical person, or cause him to conclude that Christianity is an

airy-fairy abstraction or convince him that Christians are too clever-by-half, or all three. Any presentation of the good news of Jesus has to pass the test which he did: 'the poor have the good news preached to them'; 'the common people heard him gladly.' To offer men philosophical and theological niceties is to offer a stone instead of bread. There is much to be said for the sturdy layman who scorned the theological experts before the Council of Nicaea with the remark that Christ did not 'teach us dialectics, art, or vain subtleties, but simplemindedness which is preserved by faith and good works.' Needless to say, the pundits ignored him.[11]

Living on capital

Avoiding propositional truth is, in any case, not at all easy. There is an existing stock of Christian language, thought and symbol, which arises from propositional formulations and from the accounts of Jesus which circulated in the early church and are known to us through the New Testament. Unfortunately, the 'commitment only' approach seems often to depend for its impact on this common Christian frame of reference. But if we abandon the actuality of this material, we cannot honestly call on its emotional and conceptual resources. If we do not know what happened at the crucifixion, what right have we to talk of Jesus 'sacrificing himself'? If we cannot be persuaded that Jesus' words are probably genuine, what difference in kind is left between 'Father, forgive them; they do not know what they are doing' and Sydney Carton in *A Tale of Two Cities*: 'It is a far, far better thing that I do, than I have ever done'?[12]

The impact of the phrase 'God is the ground of being' depends upon this residual Christian consciousness. It raises all the overtones of Christian assurance – 'All my hope on God is founded.' But the sentence really means that what underlies, in some sense, everything, is given by us the label 'God'. 'God' is a name for ultimate reality. 'All my hope on ultimate reality is founded' could be a serious self-commitment, but it has neither the rhythm of Robert Bridges' translation nor the emotional impact of Joachim Neander's German original.[13] And there is also the terrifying concept in Germanic thinking, of ground – '*grund*' – as the antithesis of chaos – '*ungrund*'. The apparent security of 'ground of being' is, thus, revealed as a defiant credo that absoluteness is somewhere in the collapse of everything into the black-hole of nothingness. Once more this has clearly something to say about faith being central to religion, but new concepts really need a new set of words and symbols if they are to be honest to themselves and to what they seek to replace.

Facing the facts

Honesty to traditional Christianity is, furthermore, not only a question of refusing to exploit its historic capital. It is a question of facing its original factual appeal. There is no reason to doubt that the first disciples believed and preached that they had seen an actual risen Jesus. It is arrogance in the extreme to decide that they were rationalizing their feelings about Jesus, asserting a psychological conviction when they were really aware that his corpse was still in the tomb. It sounds very well to write of the resurrection:

> [The disciples] believed it, not because it was well documented or conclusively attested, but because they came to see that it just had to be true.
>
> If Jesus was the One whom they had come to believe he was, if God was not only in this man in a unique and once and for all way, but through him was also doing something unique and once and for all, for all mankind in all places and all time, time past and still to come as well as time present, then it had to be.
>
> That they found him to be alive was, therefore, inevitable.

But this is to found the Christian church on schizoid delusions. Does it really do justice to apostolic preaching?

> You begged as a favour the release of a murderer, and killed him who led the way to life. But God raised him from the dead; of that we are witnesses.
>
> God raised him to life the third day, and allowed him to appear, not to the whole people, but to witnesses whom God had chosen in advance – to us who ate and drank with him after he rose from the dead.

And is it true to Paul?

> If Christ was not raised, then our good news is null and void, and so is your faith; and we turn out to be lying witnesses for God, because we bore witness that he raised Christ to life.

When the early Christians celebrated the eucharist, what meaning did it have outside the context of their belief in the death, resurrection and impending return of an actual Jesus? Even more, what meaning now attaches to this cult act if we demythologize our Christianity?[14]

The challenge of primitive Christianity is nowhere better seen than in the character of faith as it was then understood. Faith was existential, but it was no existential leap of despair. It was akin to the leap of utter abandonment when the child jumps into the arms of his parent; he knows he will be caught. The stress which Jesus placed upon the father-son analogy to explain the relationship of God to man, the constant theme of his parables – being called, found, welcomed, rescued – his consciousness of having a saving mission from God to men, all this bathes New Testament Christianity in the light of certainty. Nor is this emphasis missing even in the earliest evidence we have. Paul's letter to Christians in Galatia opens squarely with a reference to Christ 'who sacrificed himself for our sins, to rescue us out of this present age of wickedness, as our God and Father willed.' I Thessalonians comes to its climax in the declaration that 'he died for us, so that we, awake or asleep, might live in company with him. Therefore, hearten one another, fortify one another'.[15]

Faith is response to the 'truth' and the truth is 'good news'. Hope and faith are both grounded in the saving acts of God. To abandon the life, death and resurrection of Jesus as an event in history is to abandon Christianity. It is cowardice to cling to a faith once we have denied its origins. If we cannot be sufficiently sure about these, then integrity demands that Christianity go into liquidation. It would certainly retain immense value in symbol, in story and in the insights it gives into the human condition. But it would no longer be 'true'. Attempts to perpetuate a form of belief by dissecting an 'ultimate' truth from the revelation of Christ in history, leave us with a corpse. It would be better to inter the body and pass on.

The need to have 'faith in' something, not merely 'faith', the need to speak to all men, not just an elite, the need to be true to the origins of Christianity – all these challenge the retreat from a Christianity of truths to a Christianity of nothing but discipleship. Both are essential; one without the other is a pretence. Without discipleship, doctrines are arid propositions to be recited parrot-fashion; without truths, commitment is purely subjective. In one of his most powerful and enduring images, Jesus linked together the message and the response:

What then of the man who hears these words of mine? He is like a man who had the sense to build his house on rock. The rain came down, the floods rose, the wind blew, and beat upon that house; but it did not fall, because its foundations were on rock.

But what of the man who hears these words of mine and does not act upon them? He is like a man who was foolish enough to build his house on sand. The rain came down, the floods rose, the wind blew, and beat upon that house; down it fell with a great crash.[16]

Notes and references

1 *Calender of State Papers Spanish, 1554–1558*, no. 415.

2 Luke 16:31.

3 *Christian Believing*, ed. M.F.Wiles, SPCK, 1976, p. 37.

4 *Ibid.* p. 1.

5 *Ibid.* pp. 37, 130.

6 P.Tillich, *The Shaking of the Foundations*, Penguin Books, 1962, p. 65.

7 I.Henderson, *Rudolph Bultmann*, Lutterworth Press, 1965, p. 13.

8 R.Bultmann to the Sheffield Industrial Mission, trans. M.Jackson, in *Prism*, June 1963.

9 *The Times*, 20 April, 1976.

10 Matthew 7:21; *The Times*, 7 February, 1976.

11 Mark 12:37; Luke 7:22; K.S.Latourette, *History of Christianity*, Eyre and Spottiswoode, 1954, p. 154.

12 Luke 23:24; Charles Dickens, *A Tale of Two Cities*, final sentence.

13 Joachim Neander, *'Meine Hoffnung stehet feste'*, trans. Robert Bridges.

14 G.Abraham-Williams, 'Something happened that day' in *The Baptist Times*,

15 April, 1976; Acts 3:15; 10:40–41; 1 Corinthians 15:14–15.

15 Galatians 1:4; 1 Thessalonians 5:11.

16 Matthew 7:24–27.

Conclusion

The fire of history

History and historical theory – finding out what happened in the past and asking what 'finding out' means or achieves – are two areas which are rarely considered together. Most historians are content to practise their craft and to leave the epistemology to theorists who are very rarely historians. Even when a historian does essay a philosophical theme, it is normally separate from his research work. But the Christian cannot find refuge in either wilful myopia or schizophrenia; like the Marxist, he is obliged by personal commitment to an overall view of the historical process and to test his beliefs as they apply in particular instances.

To stand on empiricism is to stand on open ground, a target for attack, but it can equally be on firm ground. And the Christian historian is on firm ground. A modest confidence in the reliability of the evidence on which his faith is built; an acceptance of the humility which allows that we cannot comprise all things within rationalistic naturalism; a quiet insistence on the distinctiveness of Christ; an understanding of purpose which sees it in terms of individual response to God rather than mass expression through either organized church or organized state; an awareness of a morality in human affairs which is inherent to the progress of men through time: these are strong positions to hold. The Christian does not believe as a consequence of these historical positions; belief touches the heart. But because he tries his faith in the historical fire, he can hold it without reproach.

Part 2

THE CHRISTIAN FAITH
IN HISTORY

Chapter 9

The challenge of the past

When Dionysius, the classical historian, gave his famous definition that history is 'philosophy derived from examples', he was claiming a didactic value for the subject which few would now accept. But the second term of his definition remains as true today as ever it was; history exists ultimately in specific examples and nowhere else. However we may generalize and whatever we attempt in the way of hypothesis, we have always to answer to the particular. Thus no discussion of the relationship between history and Christianity can be complete without 'examples', and this is the challenge taken up in the second part of this book.

Sometimes the challenge is a positive one, to show a spiritual dimension to past events which are normally explained in exclusively materialist terms. One such would be the Reformation, another the record of missionary work in the nineteenth and twentieth centuries. At other times the task is a negative one, to examine instances where a popular orthodoxy writes off Christian belief. This is most notable in the connection between Protestantism and capitalism but it is seen in other assumptions also, such as the connection between Protestantism and the growth of nationalism.

A more familiar dimension of the problem is the past record of the church. This includes its relations with the state, its involvement in repression, its contribution to social welfare. Or again there is the matter of social and economic exploitation. The story that John Newton wrote 'Jesus the very thought of Thee with sweetness fills my breast' while on a slave-trading voyage is not true, but the association has point. The story of industrialization is equally germane. A critic wrote in 1835 against the millowners and masters who practised 'white child slavery': 'Your Dissenters may call such as these 'saints', 'pillars' and 'deacons', but...I will denounce them as *the Cardinal Legates from the Court of Hell.*'[1] As for Christianity and war, this has been the theme of countless writers, poets and painters, and more recently of theatre and film.

The standard Christian response to such questions is to point out that the organized church and genuine faith are not necessarily to be equated, and there is a good deal of force in this. Yet this defence can easily be over-employed. It is hardly reasonable to argue that time and time again the real Christian community is represented by some way-out sect which had very little significance at the time but whose eccentric views (then) put them on the side of the angels (now). All too often Christian apologists evade the evil deeds of previous believers with the claim 'of course these were not true followers of Christ'. The Christian historian must face the truth of what Jonathan Swift wrote:

> Difference in opinions hath cost many millions of lives – for instance, whether flesh be bread or bread be flesh; whether the juice of a certain berry be blood or wine.[2]

Of course there is an opposite side to the story, the devotion and service of saintly men and women in every age, but again this can be exaggerated. The Welfare State is not the sole creation of Christian concern for human need.

Given a religion which is world-wide and 2,000 years old, it would require the range, ability, leisure (and publisher) of an Edward Gibbon to attempt anything like a comprehensive survey of such issues. What is attempted here is much more limited, an exploration of a number of problems at a single period in the history of Western Europe and especially England, the period which historians call 'early modern' and which can be roughly dated as the half century before and the century-and-a-half after the Reformation. This obviously omits a great deal and there is clearly need for further enquiry and discussion. But what this limited approach can do is to examine certain of the continuing elements in the relationship of history and Christianity against the record of a particular period and region, and in studying the particular we may learn something of the general.

Attention is first given to the question of the spiritual dimension in history, as seen in the turmoil of the Reformation. Next we consider the tension between Christianity and secular authority and the varied response of Christianity to organized violence. Chapter 13 looks at Christianity and the economic system as seen in the rise of capitalism and the final discussion considers the reputation the Christian church has for repression.

Notes and references

1 Richard Oastler, quoted in U.Henriques, *The Early Factory Acts and their Enforcement*, Historical Association, 1971, p. 6 n.2.
2 Jonathan Swift, *Gulliver's Travels*, Oxford University Press, 1948, p. 304.

Chapter 10

The Reformation:
God against himself?

Christian belief and historical enquiry meet dramatically and decisively in the Reformation. One of the handful of events which have been truly epoch-making in European history, it is for the Christian a crisis, not in ecclesiastical organization so much as in human awareness of God. It is also an embarrassment. Catholic burned Protestant, Protestant killed Catholic, all to the glory of God.

What should we say about this, and what did God think about it? A hundred years ago an evangelical Protestant would have had no doubts. The Protestant martyrs (in England, Cranmer, Ridley, Latimer and the others) were the good guys; Thomas More, Edmund Campion and the Roman Catholic martyrs were the bad guys – earnest but misguided, blind and fighting against the truth. J.A.Wylie could introduce his *History of Protestantism* thus:

> Protestantism is a Divine graft on the intellectual and moral nature of man, whereby new vitalities and forces are introduced into it, and the human stem yields henceforth a nobler fruit. It is the descent of a heaven-born influence which allies itself with all the instincts and powers of the individual, with all the laws and cravings of society, and which, quickening both the individual and the social being into new life, and directing their efforts to nobler objects, permits the highest development of which humanity is capable, and the fullest possible accomplishment of all its grand ends. In a word, Protestantism is revived Christianity.[1]

More notable men than Dr Wylie agreed. Carlyle, for instance, wrote of Protestantism as 'the sacred cause of God's light and truth against the Devil's falsity and darkness'.[2] Today, however, the distinct Christian blessing of the Reformation is less obvious.

Growing uncertainty
In the first place it has been undermined by historical enquiry.

The assumption that the pre-Reformation church was uniformly corrupt is now recognized as exaggerated. The spiritual desert of the fifteenth century seems less obvious in the face of what we know about personal piety and charity, especially as shown in the wills people drew up. Indulgence-selling which Luther attacked was, we now know, an abuse perpetrated by dishonest salesmen. Tetzel certainly said 'As soon as your money chinks in the bowl, Up into heaven springs the soul', but it is equally certain that he said it without authority and contrary to the teaching of the church. There is also a feeling that the role of the Protestant heroes was somewhat equivocal. Philip of Hesse figures in Dr Wylie's history as a good soldier of Jesus Christ. To historians fully aware of his bigamous marriage and Luther's complicity, Philip may seem a hypocrite using religion for his own ends, and Luther a sycophant, bending the gospel to the dictates of his masters.

What was done in the name of religion now sickens us. Religious war, Christian steeped in the blood of Christian, appears a blasphemy. Equally disgusting is persecution, whether the treatment of More and the English Carthusians or the murder of William Tyndale. The genocide perpetrated against the Bohemians by the Habsburgs seems as lamentable as the fury of the English against the Irish. Cromwell's deliberate and satisfied roasting alive of Catholics at Drogheda or the Lutheran soldiers' sack of Rome now rank as atrocities no less than the Massacre of St Bartholomew or the brutalities of the Council of Blood.

Research has also exposed the social blindness of the reformers. The Evangelical and Reformed churches taught charity, but they left obvious evil unchallenged. We are hardly endeared by Luther's savage command to the German nobility faced with a peasant uprising, to 'smite, slay and stab, everyone who can, secretly or openly, remembering that nothing can be more poisonous, hurtful or devilish than a rebel'.[3] The reformers identified themselves all too often with the status quo and where social tradition was concerned they were deaf to the scriptures. There are few less elevating spectacles than the rallying of Lutherans to Münster to assist the Catholic bishop to wipe out a socially dangerous nest of Anabaptists.

The evident benefits of the Reformation are also less apparent. Macaulay was convinced of the disastrous influence of the later Catholic church:

Throughout Christendom, whatever advance has been made in knowledge, in freedom, in wealth, and in the arts of life, has been made in spite of her, and has everywhere been in inverse proportion to her power.[4]

Modern scholars are now aware of the dark legacy of Protestantism. While the Pandora's box opened by the reformers probably did not include modern capitalism, as Max Weber and R.H. Tawney would have us believe, it did include the seeds of Nietzsche and the omnicompetent secular state.

At the same time we are more aware of the complexity of the Reformation. Gordon Rupp has drawn attention to the contrast between the volume on the Reformation in the *Cambridge Modern History* of 1902 and in the *New Cambridge Modern History* of 1958. Luther and the German Reformation have declined from 20 per cent in 1902 to 8 per cent in 1958; Calvin has been reduced from thirty-five pages to seven. In their place have come social, economic and intellectual topics of great weight, and the next volume has the significant title of *Counter Reformation and Price Revolution*. Wylie had no doubts about the primacy of the religious issue:

> Protestantism is the master; Charles V is but the servant...All men and things exist for the Reformation. It is the Power that originates, that controls and that extorts the service of all around it. Everyone who has eyes to see and a heart to understand, must acknowledge that Protestantism stands at the very centre of the field.[5]

But today, the eyes of the historians see something different. All would tell the story of the Reformation with the social pressure of an age of ambition, the interest of the princes, the changing economic patterns, the spread of education, the printing press, hostility to church wealth and power, the new Renaissance ideas, all well to the forefront of the story. For many writers, these *are* the story.

The spiritual vigour of the pre-Reformation church, reformers who are no longer seen through ecclesiastically tinted spectacles, religious war and persecution, the ignoring of inequity in society, the doubtful benefits of the Reformation and the complexity of the problem: all this makes us forsake the simple vision of the past.

Breaking barriers

But old certainties have not simply been undermined by historical investigation. In the past seventy years Protestants and Catholics have each become aware of brethren in Christ on the other side of the confessional front-line. For years the denominations maintained an I-You relationship expressed in mutual anathemas of what they took the other to be. To the Protestant, the Catholic was a bogey, not a real person; to the Catholic, the Protestant was a devil, not a man, and similar suspicion divided Protestant and Protestant. A church was 'a little garden walled around'; the person over the wall was a potential intruder, not a fellow man, in his own garden, enjoying the same sun sent by the same God.

Gradually I-You has changed to I-Thou. Within Protestant churches a high degree of mutual acceptance has been achieved. The tone is the tone of John Wesley: 'I ask not… "Are you of my church, or my congregation?"…My only question is this, "Is thine heart right as my heart is with thy heart?"…If it be, give me thy hand.'[6]

Now relations are being built up across the Catholic/non-Catholic divide, with less mutual acceptance as yet, but complete tolerance and recognition. What then becomes of the Reformation? The meeting of Catholic Christian and Protestant Christian cannot be just in our own day; it must be an encounter in history. And if the Protestant finds true spirituality, godly devotion and a commitment to truth among those hostile to Protestantism, if he sees what he might, in religious terms, describe as the Spirit of God at work on the Catholic side of the schism, then he must revise his picture of the Reformation.

For the non-Christian historian the problem, of course, does not exist. First, he is able to dismiss many of the troublesome features of the Reformation as evidence of the general state of men's thinking at the time. The social conservatism of reform, the deference to the prince, the trust in torture and persecution, all are evidence of the different attitudes of a different age – *'autres temps, autres moeurs'*. The force of this must be admitted. To condemn Martin Luther for not being General Booth is whiggery of the first order. The moral for the Christian is the ease with which good men can become conformed to their social and intellectual environment. But not all can be explained in this way.

The Reformation is not just a sixteenth century phenomenon. It is, so Christians believe, an event of spiritual significance. To a Catholic it has been the fiery trial which purified the church, a fight against the hosts of hell; to evangelical Protestants is has been a stride forward by the eternal gospel. Yet this fight, this stride, crushed thousands into misery and death. So long as we cherished the old stereotypes, the misery and death could be explained as the consequence of the devil resisting the truth. But what if the Spirit of God was on both sides?

The non-Christian, too, sees no difficulty in good men being misguided, misunderstanding each other, doing evil for the best of motives, dealing out death in the course of 'idiot controversies' about 'theological nonsense'; this is what men are like. The standard reaction of the ecumenical movement to the past is akin to this, 'Lord, forgive us for our blindness and folly'. But this will not do for the historian who accepts the Christian position on history, that God is in control of and is active in his world. If it was all one horrible mistake which can only put us in sackcloth and ashes, it says little for God.

The new ecumenical spirit leads us to recognize the existence of committed disciples of Christ, 'converted' individuals, irrespective of denomination. If this is so, then probably there were 'converted' people on both sides of the Reformation divide. And when we find them, what becomes of the work of God which Christians have always seen in the Reformation? The Old Kaspars of tradition will keep affirming, 'It was a famous victory', but we shall ask with Little Wilhelmine and Peterkin:

> Tell us all about the war,
> And what they fought each other for,
>   And what good came of it at last.[7]

Jesuit spirituality

It does not take long to discover that a simple 'truth versus darkness' version of the Reformation does break down. If any group of men in history have seemed to be implacably hostile to the Reformation it is the Jesuits. Ignatius Loyola, their founder, came from a conventionally religious, noble family in the Basque lands of Northern Spain. A soldier wounded at Pamplona in 1521, he suffered a long convalescence during which he had to suffer even more by the absence of all books except the *De Vita Christi* by Ludwig of Saxony, and a volume of saints' lives. The *De Vita Christi* is not just a biography of Jesus. It is designed as a spiritual exercise to encourage devotion to and imitation of Christ; it includes theology, spiritual and moral teaching, and prayers. Under its influence Loyola was changed. He abandoned his old life and all his wealth and became a wandering ascetic, fasting, praying, tending the sick and preaching.

Like Luther, Ignatius had a great consciousness of the majesty of God and of his own sinfulness. Unlike Luther, however, the release did not come through study of the Bible – Loyola at this stage was poorly educated – but through mysticism and visions, a type of religious experience with a long and powerful tradition. It was this practice of inner communion with God which was to produce his *Spiritual Exercises*. Where Luther wrestled to understand, Loyola accepted and pondered until his mind was alive with the feeling of God. He went on a one-man mission to convert the Muslims, came back and went to school. He then became a wandering preacher, suspected by the Inquisition and more than once in jail. Next he worked among the students of Paris and on 15 August 1534 he and six others founded a society to conduct a mission in Palestine or wherever the Pope directed – no organization, no method, no money, it was a faith mission.

The heart of the enterprise was the *Spiritual Exercises*, a book reminiscent of the *Imitation of Christ* by Thomas à Kempis. It is a series of specific meditations on the life and death of Christ, practical and ascetic, for those who wish to undertake a spiritual retreat intended to transform both life and character. It sets out to produce a following of Christ, not in mental experience only, but in daily action. Loyola's sequence for examining the conscience before God was 'Give Thanks', 'Seek Light', 'Self-examination', 'Grief', 'Set Out', and has obvious similarities with Protestant books of spiritual direction. Puritans, in particular, had much use for such systems and there is even one case of direct connection between the Jesuits and the English non-conformists; the 'cleaned-up' Protestant version of a directory written by the arch-Jesuit, Father Parsons, was responsible for the conversion of Richard Baxter, the great puritan divine.

The Protestant-Catholic divide is crossed in doctrine as well as devotion. Loyola's book shows that his deepest convictions were the sovereignty of God, the redemption wrought by him through Christ and the conviction that human beings find the meaning and fullness of life only through Christ and through full surrender to God. The vision and enjoyment of God was what God intended for man and what should be the purpose of man's life. Luther's vision was identical, and Calvin's also. It is appropriate that in the year in which Loyola and his friends took their vows, Calvin should have been writing the classic of the Protestant Reformation, his *Institutes of the Christian Religion* (first published 1536).

In 1540, Loyola's group were established as the Company of Jesus, and when he died in 1556 the order had grown to 1,000 and was world-wide. Ignatius was its General, its 'home director', organizing, training, in charge of postings and very practical about hygiene and medical reports.

The most appealing of his colleagues was another Spaniard, Francis Xavier, an aristocrat whom Loyola won by personal influence when they shared a room at Paris. A member of the original group, he was sent at a day's notice and at the age of thirty-five to convert India. He evangelized among the hard-bitten European traders of Goa who shamelessly exploited the Indians, founded a college and recruited for the society. Then he undertook a two-year mission to the nominally Christian Paravas in south-eastern India, during which he learned enough of the language to teach this despised, low-caste people the Apostles' Creed, the Ten Commandments, the Lord's Prayer and other prayers. He worked especially among the children and the region remains predominantly Roman-Catholic to this day.

Next Xavier turned to the fishermen of Travancore, then to Ceylon, Malacca and the Moluccan Islands before returning to India. His linguistic feats were prodigious, and we hear of him singing a Malay hymn in the jungle at Amboina in order to attract the natives. In 1549 he reached Japan, where he began an astonishingly successful mission, during which he walked to Kyoto, 480 km/300 miles barefoot, up to his knees in snow. Francis Xavier was only in Japan for two years, but by 1582 there were 200 churches and 150,000 converts. His next objective was China, and in 1552 he went to an island off the South China coast, hoping to secure entry to the mainland. He died there, apparently of exposure, at the age of forty-six. The comparison with later Protestant missionary heroes such as William Carey or Henry Martyn is compelling.

A third Jesuit example is the Englishman, Edmund Campion. Born in 1540, he became a brilliant scholar and an Oxford don who in 1566 was chosen by his colleagues to address Queen Elizabeth on her visit to the university. His Catholic convictions led him to resign from Oxford, and he went in 1569 to Ireland, and from there to the continent, to the new Catholic college for English exiles in Douai. Joining the Jesuits in 1573, Campion first worked in Prague but was recalled in 1579 to become part of the project to convert his native country.

The need for a Christian ministry to England was obvious. The numerous religious changes since the break with Rome in 1533 had left the nation bewildered, and the latest Anglican settlement of 1559 appeared only a naked political compromise, not yet clothed in the garment of reason woven by Hooker or imbued with the life of a John Donne or a George Herbert. From the reforming camp, the puritans saw the need, from the Catholic camp, the secular missionary priests and then the Jesuits. Edmund Campion and Robert Parsons were chosen to blaze the trail.

The two arrived in England in June 1580 for what was, in Campion's case, a hectic thirteen months of secret evangelism. On the move every two days, busy reconciling and converting the lapsed and the lost to the Catholic church, giving spiritual advice, setting up and writing for an illegal press – a copy of one of his pamphlets was put on each chair at the Oxford Commemoration of 1581 – Campion evangelized in Berkshire, Oxfordshire and Northamptonshire, through Nottinghamshire and the West Riding into Lancashire. He was captured in July 1581, tortured, tried, and on 1 December drawn to the gallows at Tyburn, hanged and quartered. It so happens that to prevent the circulation of false information if he were captured, Campion had tossed off a statement about his mission, to be used in an emergency. Towards the close, he writes of the Jesuits:

> We have made a league...cheerfully to carry the cross you shall lay upon us, and never to despair your recovery, while we have a man left to enjoy your Tyburn, or to be racked with your torments, or consumed with your prisons. The expense is reckoned, the enterprise is begun; it is of God, it cannot be withstood. So the faith was planted, so it must be restored.[8]

Here we surely have the authentic note of Christian conviction.

Now no doubt Loyola, Xavier and Campion regarded Luther as evil, and Luther's followers, Calvin and his followers and the other Protestants all reciprocated. Equally, a Protestant today will be unhappy with some of the Jesuit message, but he may also be unhappy with parts (admittedly a lesser proportion) of Luther and Calvin. The Jesuits rejected Luther's truth that 'faith alone' saves a man; some Calvinists verged on rejecting the truth that salvation is for all. From a twentieth-century evangelical position it seems that both rejections were wrong and unnecessary. But it is hard for a Christian today to deny that the Jesuits, no less than the Protestants were committed Christians filled with the Spirit of God.

Hunger for reform

What, then, are we to make of the sixteenth century in ecumenical terms, with God fighting himself? The answer, it may be suggested, lies in the fifteenth century, in the much maligned medieval church. It is true that the organized church was gradually moving away from the laity and becoming a body run by and for priests – at a high level, men engaged primarily in the work of the state and only secondarily the Christian community, and at a lower level, men frequently ill-educated and ill-informed. Aberrant forms of the Christian faith were widespread, based upon the elaboration of the doctrine of purgatory and were believed by the intelligent as well as the ignorant. In England the great exponent of such ideas was none other than Thomas More, a statesman with a European reputation as a scholar. The consequence of this was a great emphasis on the mass as a mechanical device which, by sheer arithmetical repetition, could deliver the souls of the departed from purgatory.

Hundreds of priests lived merely by saying masses for the dead. Humphrey Coningsby, a judge who died in 1535, arranged for five 'trentals', sets of thirty masses, to be said as soon as possible after his death and two masses and the *dirige*, or matins for the departed, at all the churches he had attended. But that was modest. Thomas Kebell, another lawyer, who died in 1500, stated in his will:

> I will that a thousand masses and as many times *placebo* [vespers for the departed] and *dirige* to be said immediately after my decease, and every priest to have 4d., the sum whereof amounteth to £16 13s 4d., or else so many trentals as a thousand masses cometh to, by the discretion of my executors.[9]

In other words, 4d each or by the trental. In addition, a priest was to say the full office of the dead and extra prayers, every day for seven years. Related aberrations were superstitious pilgrimages and the cult of relics. Those collected by Luther's patron, the Elector of Saxony, earned the visitor more than 100,000 years exemption from purgatory. Among the 17,000 items were no fewer than 204 pieces of the Holy Innocents, the Bethlehem children slaughtered by Herod soon after the birth of Christ, a millennium and a half before.

Yet this is only part of the story. What made these weaknesses seem so serious – many, after all, were not new – was the growth of a higher level of Christian aspiration. Men and women wanted more from their religion and pressure built up because, by and large, the church was failing to meet this need. Luther's spiritual plight was not unique. The evidence of religious interest is to be seen most simply in the eager way the Christian world took to the printing press. New religious initiatives show the same concern. Some were taken by higher clerics, men like Cardinal Ximenes in

Spain or Bishop Barozzi in Padua; others are found in monastic communities – Luther himself is a product of the order of reformed Augustinian Friars.

There was also a great deal of self-help outside the church: the heretical movements of Lollardy and Hussitism can even be seen in this light. Among the orthodox, the Oratory of Divine Love grew up in Southern Europe, and in Northern Europe the Brethren of the Common Life with their *devotio moderna*. Both movements rejected traditional notions that the ideal for the Christian was ascetic monastic seclusion. They looked instead for a way to live the life of the Christian believer in the everyday world. The Brethren, for example, attempted to return to the practice of primitive Christian discipleship, based on a study of the Bible. They lived in communities and the organized church with its sacraments and scholasticism had little relevance for them. The great classic of the movement, the *Imitation of Christ* has scarcely anything to say of the church, but is heavily dependent on scripture and is a guide to mystical experience, not liturgy.

Doubt about the value of monastic vows was found in the highest circles. Jean Gerson, the chancellor of the University of Paris, set up his sisters as a religious community in the home. At lower levels doubt verged on denial. Gerard Groote, a founder of the Brethren, said: 'To love God and worship him is religion, not the taking of special vows.'[10] Others effectively rejected the church altogether. Francesco Datini of Prato, a Florentine merchant who died in 1410, left a large fortune to the poor in such a way that neither the church nor individual clerics had any say in its use.

On the positive side there was the great interest in preaching, with Savonarola the most noted figure. There was also the emergence, in part from the Brethren of the Common Life, of Christian Humanism and, supremely, the achievements of Erasmus of Rotterdam. With allies such as Thomas More and John Colet, Erasmus proclaimed the need for a real scriptural religion, and made that possible by producing a new text of the Greek New Testament which revolutionized biblical interpretation. Luther himself acknowledged his debt to Erasmus, and Erasmus initially welcomed Luther and always believed that the reformer was right on many matters.

The conclusion is obvious. By about 1500, Europe was experiencing one of the periodic revivals which have characterized the history of Christianity and which, in many respects, was long overdue. In different ways and in different places, people were taking a renewed and firmer, a more personal grasp on their faith.

To the Christian historian it may well seem clear that God was at work in exactly the way a Christian view of history would suggest.

Reform and reaction

What went wrong? Reform necessarily implies a movement against a status quo. As the spirit of Christian revival spread, it came up against the forces of secularism, entrenched in church and state. The story is well known: clerical authorities in Germany who were anxious to shut Luther up; a pope who had the considerations of an Italian prince foremost in his mind; careerists among the cardinals and clerics; a king of England who identified the church and himself; Spanish rulers who made the church the instrument of national unity; laymen who wanted church wealth; princes who saw religion as a counter in the game of independence. On this construction, the reformers, although we may now label them Catholic and Protestant, were on one side, and the politiques and the traditionalists on the other. Henry VIII, the pope and Charles V, against More, Loyola and Luther. In consequence, reform in some places broke away from the church and the reaction within the church to reform produced the Counter-Reformation. But the ultimate root of Protestantism and revived Catholicism was the same, the revival of 1500.

This is more than one of the neat paradoxical patterns historians enjoy. It is fundamental to an understanding of the spirit of those involved. We have seen Roman Catholic Christians reacting to the religious vacuum of Elizabethan England. They were equalled in zeal by the puritans, especially for the conversion of 'the dark corners of the land'.

> I know not my danger in writing these things. I see you my dear and native country perish, it pitieth me. I come with the rope around my neck to save you, howsoever it goes with me, I labour that you may have the Gospel preached among you, though it cost me my life, I think it well bestowed.

Compare the following:

> My charge is, of free cost to preach the Gospel, to minister the Sacraments, to instruct the simple, to reform sinners, to confute errors – in brief to cry alarm spiritual against foul vice and proud ignorance wherewith many my dear Countrymen are abused.

Not only the language, the emotion, the sentiments, but also the motivation is the same, a desire to bring men to commitment to

Jesus Christ. Yet the first is from the pen of an obscure Welsh evangelist, John Penry, the second from the pen of Edmund Campion. Campion was executed by Elizabeth's government in 1581, John Penry in 1593.[11]

By the 1580s, what had originated in a single Christian revival was hopelessly split into opposing factions. Or perhaps 'split' is an inadequate word to describe the virulence of the Catholic-Protestant confrontation. Each side progressively defined its position against the other. The Roman Catholic church wilfully rejected the light of Lutheran reform by defining its doctrine at the Council of Trent in a deliberately anti-Protestant sense; matters which had previously been open to discussion now became articles of faith. The Anglican church defined its tenets against Catholics and Anabaptists. The Reformed and the Evangelical communions lined up against each other and against Rome. Divisions were exacerbated and deliberately emphasized. So Jesuits became the bitter enemies of the puritans, and vice-versa. Missionaries were hounded down by their fellow Christians; men who wanted to tell the ignorant that Christ died for them, tortured and slaughtered other men who wanted to tell the ignorant that Christ died for them.

It may be objected, of course, that this is an oversimplification; Catholic and Protestant were and are deeply divided on what constitutes truth and error. This is certainly so on some issues, but this division was not inevitable from the start. The tide of Christian revival and reform was broken into a chaos of conflicting currents by the rocks of unbelief, represented by the organized state and the organized church. It is impossible to imagine the 'might-have-been'. Suppose the fervour which bled away in religious war had followed Francis Xavier to the mission field...

Challenge and conflict

To see the Reformation in this way makes it possible to see in it an act of God for which Catholic and Protestant alike have cause to give thanks. But one further term in the progression seems to be required. If the inception of the revival is attributed to God, does the outcome imply that he gave up or lost control?

If the previous discussion of the way God can be understood to fulfil a purpose in history is sound, then his activity takes place principally in and through his new community. The growth of that community, either in size or in quality of life, must always be in the context of, and in reaction to what already exists. Hence any revival necessarily implies challenge and conflict. The problems of the sixteenth century church were, perhaps, centuries old, dating back to the shallowness of the original conversion from paganism in large areas of the continent outside the Roman world. There is much to be said for the view that the Reformation was the non-Romanized north of Europe appropriating the gospel for itself. Revival was also against the legacy of the church's history, notably the absorption of the higher clergy into politics and government, even into princely office. The universal identification of church and state had an inevitably deleterious effect. Mary Tudor was certainly the most positively Christian of all her family, and perhaps the most devout of English monarchs, but her influence upon Catholic Christianity could not have been more baleful.

The Christian metaphor is one of light shining in darkness and the darkness never extinguishing it. What makes the matter complex is that darkness and light are not in separate zones but that dark and light are within each Christian. The revival of 1500 was, like all revivals, a challenge to each Christian personally; with personality, background, intelligence, conditioning so different from man to man it is easy to see why revival would have disparate and contradictory effects. There is no surprise in a Luther splitting with Zwingli over the mystery of the sacrament, no surprise in a Loyola sharing much of Calvin's theology but dedicated to destroying Calvinism. If every Christian had been infinitely Christlike, if every Christian had been wholly liberated from the social and economic system, if every Christian had been humble enough and brave enough to see that doctrinal formulations and human logic give an approximation to the truth, not the truth itself, then there would have been no conflict. There would have been heaven!

Ecumenical and convinced

In this chapter we have tried to face the issue that if a Christian believes that God does act in history, then he needs to face up to the problem of God acting in the Reformation. The conclusion is that God can only be held to act if he acted ecumenically, in Catholic and Protestant alike. The saints of the Catholic church in the Reformation and the founders of Protestantism are the common heritage of all twentieth-century Christians. Already this feeling exists within the Protestant community. Cranmer is no more the exclusive property of Anglicans than John Bunyan is of Baptists and Independents, and this despite the burning of Baptists by Cranmer, the hanging of Independents by Anglicans, or the repression of Anglicans by Presbyterians and Independents when their turn came, or the inevitable Anglican revenge. This projection has now to be made between Protestant and Catholic. We have to be ready to consider that Thomas More as well as his great adversary William Tyndale, Martin Luther as well as Ignatius Loyola, Francis Xavier and John Calvin, John Penry and Edmund Campion could all be among the faithful.

The ecumenical response to the Reformation requires a broadness of sympathy and a certainty of position. Wesley has already advised us of the first, he does the same on the second. 'A catholic [ecumenical] spirit', he wrote, 'is not speculative latitudinarianism', it is rooted in settled convictions; Catholic belief will be no less Catholic, Protestant conviction no less Protestant. Nor is an ecumenical spirit 'practical latitudinarianism'; it is rooted in the conviction that one form of worship is 'scriptural and rational'; it does not imply a rejection of particular churchmanship. But from this firm base it reaches out to all who believe in the Lord Jesus Christ, who love God and man, who are careful to abstain from evil and zealous of good works'.[13]

To be convinced is not necessarily to be partisan. Again to quote Edmund Campion:

> I have no more to say but to recommend your case and mine to Almighty God, the Searcher of Hearts, who send us His grace, and set us at accord before the day of payment, to the end we may at last be friends in heaven, when all injuries shall be forgotten.[12]

Notes and references

1 J.A.Wylie, *The History of Protestantism*, Cassell, Petter and Galpin, i.2.

2 *Ibid*.i.iii.

3 E.G.Rupp and B.Drewery, *Martin Luther*, E.Arnold, 1970, p. 122.

4 T.B.Macaulay, *The History of England from the Accession of James II*, Dent, 1906 edn., i.44.

5 Wylie, *History of Protestantism*, i.622.

6 John Wesley, *Forty-four Sermons*, Epworth Press, 1944, pp. 447–48, 450.

7 Robert Southey, 'The Battle of Blenheim'.

8 A.C.Southern, *English Recusant Prose 1559–82*, Sands, 1950, p. 155.

9 Prerogative Court of Canterbury Wills, 3 Moone.

10 M.Aston, *The Fifteenth Century*, Thames and Hudson 1968, p. 157.

11 John Penry, *An Exhortation unto the Governors and People of Wales*, 1588, p. 63; Southern, *English Recusant Prose*, p. 154.

12 Wesley, *Forty-four Sermons*, pp. 453, 455; Southern, *English Recusant Prose*, p. 155.

Chapter 11

The state: compromise and challenge in England, 1530–1640

On 8 December 1576, the first Saturday in Advent, Edmund Grindal, Archbishop of Canterbury, sat in his study at Lambeth, writing a letter to the queen, refusing to obey orders. Elizabeth I had instructed him to suppress 'prophesyings', meetings of clergymen to study the Bible. He could not, he said, obey with a safe conscience and without offence to God.

> Bear with me, I beseech you, Madam, if I choose rather to offend your earthly majesty than to offend against the heavenly majesty of God.[1]

Elizabeth should not in religious matters 'pronounce so resolutely and peremptorily as if by authority'; she should refer such issues to her church. And, perhaps with the first lesson appointed for morning prayer that day still in his mind – 'now the Egyptians are men and not God' – he concluded 'Remember, Madam, that you are a mortal creature.'

One state – one church

This famous letter, which ruined Grindal's career, points more economically than any analysis can to the distinctive character of church-state relations in the time of the Reformation. In the Anglo-Saxon world today the separation of the church and the state is self-evident. But in the century and a half following the discovery of America and preceding the Scientific Revolution and the Enlightenment, this was not the case. The King of France was 'the Most Christian King'; the rulers of Spain, 'the Catholic Kings'; Henry VIII, 'Defender of the Faith' and Elizabeth I, 'Supreme Governor of the Church of England'. Educated opinion, of course, was well aware of the need 'to obey God rather than men', but the likelihood that this would become a real challenge was regarded as remote; if it did arise, the accepted opinion was that the Christian stance could only be that of non-co-operation.

During the religious wars of the sixteenth and the seventeenth

century, the horrid choice between taking up the sword and submitting to godlessness had actually to be faced. Christians of all
persuasions exhibited great distress and where possible contorted
themselves into some topsy-turvey posture of loyalty. When Henry
of Navarre succeeded to the French throne in 1589 his
Huguenot supporters put away the arguments of the treatise *Vin-
diciae contra Tyrannos*, and exchanged with relief the less satisfactory
justification of resistance to a godless ruler for the legitimist
arguments hitherto the watchword of their Catholic foes. Half a
century later it was the turn of the English to search for evasions.
The criticisms of 1640 and 1641 were nominally directed not at
Charles I but at ministers who, allegedly, had wrongly advised
him. Similarly, after 1642, war was waged not against the King,
but for 'King and Parliament'. Only among an aberrant minority
was any real detachment of the Christian from the state
recognized, still less accepted.

Indeed, even to talk of 'the Christian' and 'the state' is to use the
language of that minority and adopt a formulation which most
men at the time would not have understood. In the sense that virtually everybody accepted the Christian gospel as factually true,
there were no 'non-Christians'. We must, in consequence, see the
relations of church and state in terms of the interpenetration of
the one by the other. Equally we must see the religious issue not as
the church preaching to the world, but as the problem of im-
plementing an accepted belief.

Royal religion
The normative position of the Christian religion and the interpenetration of church and state was as axiomatic in England as
in the rest of Reformation Europe. There were, however, unique
features in England arising from the fact that the Reformation
there was brought about by state action rather than religious
agitation. The consequence was to subordinate the doctrine and
liturgy of English Christianity to Henry VIII's personal interpretation. In medieval times the state had gradually extended its practical authority over the church, but what was asserted after 1533
was the king's right to determine religious belief and behaviour
within his territories. By 1547, when Henry died, English men and
women were being taught a religion which was distinctively the
king's own devising.

At the heart of this was a radical reinterpretation of the nature
of the church. Instead of medieval Christendom's toleration of
local customs within an international, united institution of divine

origin, Henry asserted that unity was only metaphysical. The King's Book of 1543 declared:

> All these churches, in divers countries...be all but one holy church catholic...and the unity of these holy churches standeth not by knowledging of one governor in earth...nor is conserved by the bishop of Rome's authority or doctrine.

In consequence, political allegiance and spiritual allegiance could no longer be set one against the other.

> And every Christian man ought to...follow the particular church of that region...wherein he is born or inhabiteth. And as all Christian people...be bound to obey...Christ the only Head of the universal church, so likewise...by his commandment,...to...obey next unto himself Christian kings.[2]

The traditional Christian view had been expressed in the metaphor of the two swords – church and state each having full executive authority in distinct areas. At his trial, Thomas More entered a motion in arrest of judgement, claiming precisely that the king did not have the right to spiritual authority:

> This indictment is grounded upon an Act of Parliament directly repugnant to the laws of God and his holy Church, the supreme government of which, or of any part whereof, may no temporal prince presume by any law to take upon him, as rightfully belonging to the See of Rome, a spiritual pre-eminence by the mouth of our Saviour himself, personally present upon earth, only to St Peter and his successors, bishops of the same see, by special prerogative granted; it is therefore in law, amongst Christian men, insufficient to charge any Christian man.[3]

Subsequent Anglican apologists retreated from the notion that the king could personally define doctrine – this had been declared by the consensus of the faithful in the creeds and the first four general councils of the church – but doctrine apart, the sovereign remained in theory and practice the head of the church. The Christian commonwealth and the Christian church were coincident. As the future archbishop, John Whitgift, wrote in 1572,

> I perceive no such distinction of the commonwealth and the church that they should be counted, as it were, two several bodies, governed with divers laws and divers magistrates, except the church be linked with an heathenish and idolatrous commonwealth.

Seventeen years earlier, Thomas Cranmer had objected to being tried by a papal commission, for exactly the same reason:

> Alas, it cannot but grieve the heart of any natural subject to be accused of the king and queen of his own realm, and specially before an outward judge, or by authority coming from any person out of this realm [i.e. the pope]...As though the king and queen could not do or have justice within their own realms against their own subjects, but they must seek it at a stranger's hands in a strange land.

At his trial Cranmer said of Henry VIII:

> Every king in his own realm and dominion is supreme head and so was he, supreme head of the church of Christ in England.[4]

The significance of the redecoration of English churches during the Reformation has often been noted – religious wall paintings were whitewashed over and the royal coat of arms erected, almost in their place. In more than one church, scriptural texts were added to make the point clearer. Above one such coat of arms is a quotation from 1 Peter, 'Fear God and honour the king'; below is a text from Proverbs 'My son, fear thou the Lord and the king: and meddle not with them that are given to change: For their calamity shall rise suddenly; and who knoweth the ruin of them both?'[5] 'Fear the Lord', 'Fear the king' – these are two modes of the same statement.

It would be wrong, however, to see this submission of Christianity to the English state only in terms of titles and assertions of authority. The church had a highly important judicial machine with a wide competence especially in the field of morals and the correction of manners. Although the state did not, in general, seize the chance to effect a moral revival, it did use the church courts negatively to serve the propaganda arm of the crown. Similarly, ecclesiastical authority over books and education was employed to establish censorship and the indoctrination of the young.

The pulpit was the principal organ of public verbal communication and the church the largest regular gathering which most people attended. Hence the sermon held a vital place in the control of men's minds – as Charles I said: 'People are governed more by the pulpit than the sword in time of peace.' Clergy were told what to preach; every quarter appropriate homilies had to be read instructing the people in their duties. By the reign of Elizabeth attendance at church was enforced by state law and the church was using new catechisms to instruct the young. It is small wonder that Charles I's critic, Sir John Eliot, should agree, 'religion it is that keeps the subject in obedience.'[6]

There can be no doubt that allowing the state this special status in Christian things verged in England upon idolatry. Three days after the death of Elizabeth I, a preacher in the royal chapel said:

> So there are two excellent women, one that bare Christ [the Virgin Mary] and another that blest Christ [Anna the prophetess]. To these we may join a third that bare and blest him both. She bare him in her heart as a womb, she conceived him in faith, she brought him forth in abundance of good works.

Several times in the early seventeenth century Elizabeth was described as 'in earth the first, in heaven the second maid'.[7]

Extreme though this may seem to be, we should remember that the special status of the ruler, what Protestants called 'the godly magistrate', was accepted Europe-wide. The role of the princes in the establishment of German Lutheranism needs no more emphasis than the importance of the Habsburg emperors in the story of the Counter-Reformation. A Scots minister might remind James VI that he was 'God's silly vassal', but the majority of Europeans would not have recognized the intended slight on royal authority. Paradoxically, 'the prince is answerable to God' was a doctrine which served to free princely authority from earthly fetters, it was the maxim of divine right. Given Reformation Europe, the prince, the embodiment of the state, was bound to have a pre-eminence in the church.

The cement of society

The supremacy of the state over the church is one aspect of the story, but the interpenetration of Christianity and the community went deeper than political dogmas and their implications. The whole fabric of society was conceived of and explained in religious terms; religion and society, not just religion and the state were identified. This was true of the thought forms of society, what is commonly called the Tudor notion of order or 'the great chain of being'. The *Homily on Obedience* proclaims that God has created the universe 'in a beautiful order':

> Where there is no right order, there ariseth all abuses, carnal liberty, enormity, sin and babylonical confusion. Take away kings, princes, rulers, magistrates, judges, and such state of God's

order, no man shall ride or go by the highway unrobbed, no
man shall sleep in his own house or bed unkilled, no man shall
hold his wife, children and possessions in quietness; all things
shall be common, and there must needs follow all mischief and
utter destruction.[8]

The imposition of one uniform religious authority was axiomatic,
and the notion of self-determination in religion anathema. This is
why Roger William's book *The Bloody Tenent of Persecution* was
burned in 1644 at the order of parliament, for he had argued im-
piously that a church was a private society which did not affect
what he called 'the essence of being of' the state.

Between systems of religion and systems of government there
was, it was felt, a natural correspondence. 'A presbytery agreeth
with monarchy as God and the devil', said James I, getting his
terms reversed, while Archbishop Laud remarked that a belief in
religious equality, what he termed 'all fellows in the church', was
incompatible with monarchy. Hence an attack on the church
hierarchy threatened an attack on monarchy, and so on the whole
notion of proper deference in the community, a point expressed in
another James I aphorism, 'no bishop, no king, no nobility'.[9]

It is this function of religion as the cement of society which
explains the inclusion in the Anglican *Articles of Religion* of such od-
dities as the lawfulness of war at the order of the magistrate, the
justification of property and the propriety of oaths. These were key
elements in maintaining the status quo so the church had to teach
them as part of 'true religion'. In other words, Christianity was so
involved in the community that some of its very doctrines were
deliberately shaped by the fears of that society. And the Civil War
demonstrated that such fears had justification, as suggested in this
Cavalier song:

The mitre is down, and so is the crown,
And with them the coronet too;
Come clowns and come boys, come hobble-de-hoys,
Come females of all degree;
Stretch out your throats and bring in your votes,
And make good the anarchy.[10]

The church, the victim of authority
What all this meant for the cause of Christ is debatable and
depends to some degree upon individual definitions of what a
church should be. If we adopt Ernst Troeltsch's categories of
'church-type' Christianity, institutional, clerical, sacramental, in-

volved in society, as against the 'sect-type' Christianity of personal experience, lay, sanctified and separate from the world, the situation was obviously much nearer the former than the latter. The cost was a secularization of the faith which deprived it of any prophetic role – the church criticizing society.

The medieval church resisted Henry VIII with great courage, but it was sapped by its surrender to the crown. In the Elizabethan settlement of 1559 political considerations produced a church which satisfied nobody – 'halfly forward and more than halfly backward', what John Knox called 'a mingle-mangle'.[11] Whatever was done was done at the behest of the state, for the interests of the state. Mary's attempt to revive Catholicism was a political operation just as much as Elizabeth's attempt to discourage it. Mary used the apparatus of the church to hand over objectors to be burned. Elizabeth was more astute and in some ways more honest – she used the machinery of treason. The object was the same, the extinction of religious dissent, and the energy the same, the energy of the state.

Nor is this consequence exhibited only at national level. The role of religion in society and the nature of Tudor patronage put the fortunes of the gospel for the next two hundred years into the hands of the local men of property. For example, Sir Richard Newdigate of Arbury in Warwickshire kept a diary in the reign of Charles II which includes the fines he imposed on his servants:

> Betty Air and Sarah Haseldine, 2s 6d apiece, for going to Coton Church where I ordered them to go to Astley. This Hester shall have because she obeyed.[12]

At local level and at the centre, Christianity became the tool of authority and its victim.

On the other hand, there are few grounds for assuming that those who dissented from what the law enacted were themselves exempt from this secularizing tendency. It is notable that Roman Catholicism survived as the ideology of a certain group of traditionally-minded gentry. When the Jesuit priests arrived in the 1580s with the call to evangelize the country at whatever cost, these gentry refused to follow. Much of the appeal of radical puritanism lay in its social implications – the replacement of the existing hierarchical structure and the substitution of another giving more freedom to the family unit and more status to the 'middling sort' in society. When the puritans did escape from royal and episcopal authority to the settlements of the New World, their behaviour showed how much of the old Adam they had taken with them. The lesson is of the enervating effects of the secular penetration of Christianity, not the identification of this particular wrong turn or that.

What of the tiny minority who actually did demand the complete antithesis of Christianity and the state, notably, but not exclusively the Anabaptists? The problem here is that such a position might seem the logical conclusion to draw from some parts of the Bible but, in the sixteenth and seventeenth centuries, it was self-defeating and quite impossible as a major Christian option. Anabaptists relied in practice on the existence of an ordered society outside their communities, but at the same time refused to see that their position was a solvent of the ties that bound that society together.

It is not without significance that in England the spread of such revolutionary religious ideas was connected with the immense expansion of internal trade, especially after 1570, with a consequent growth of a wayfaring community, mobile, belonging to no settled order, rootless and radical. The great classic of the English Revolution was *The Pilgrim's Progress*, a spiritualized diary of a travelling salesman, composed by an itinerant tinker who spent years in jail for his non-conformity. By depicting Christian as a pilgrim, John Bunyan effectively abandoned the world to the devil. The pilgrim is not the prophet. However justified from scripture, the radical expression of Christianity was disqualified as unrealistic and selfish.

What is more, it got what it asked for. Henry Barrow was the much-imprisoned leader of the Elizabethan separatists, those puritans who sought independence from the state church (but not the social isolation of the Anabaptists). He attacked the established Anglican church as an

> invention of man, even that man of sin, erroneous, imposed and thrust upon their churches....Neither endeavour we to reform your Babylonish deformities....This trash we know to be devote to execration by the Lord's own irrevocable sentence; and therefore we leave the reformation of them to the Lord's visitation in judgement.

More specifically, there was in the true church no special place for the 'godly magistrate'; the prerogatives of the royal supremacy belonged to the local congregation, a point which gave the group their slogan, coined by Robert Browne, 'reformation without tarrying for any'. Hence, with perfect consistency but no charity, Barrow played into the hands of his critics by abusing the

Archbishop of Canterbury to his face, before the privy council, as 'a monster, a miserable compound,...neither ecclesiastical nor civil, even that second beast spoken of in the Revelation.'[13] So although logic was on the side of the separatists, society and the state were with reason convinced of their essential subversiveness. In 1593 the founders, Barrow and Greenwood, were hanged and with them John Penry, the most promising recruit to separation, while a statute gave the choice between conformity and exile or death.

Here we have an impasse. It was impossible for the faith to be other than the victim of the state because neither the state nor the great majority of believers could conceive of the separation of belief and citizenship. It was a conceptual block which condemned to ineffectiveness the tiny groups which did attempt that separation. The radicals were superficial when they abused state religion as a perversion of true belief; they were facing not apostasy but a deeply entrenched culture pattern.

Bringing pressure to bear

The opposite side to the story of the influence of the state and the community upon Christianity is the influence of Christianity upon the state and the community. Perhaps four distinct episodes are of special interest in England: the 1530s; the minority of Edward VI; the 'prophesyings' crisis of 1576 and attempts at moral reformation by statute.

The 'prophesyings' controversy we have already observed with Grindal's letter. Encouraging Bible studies for the clergy was an obvious way for evangelical bishops to try to raise standards in the church. Prophesyings could, of course, become a happy hunting ground for the more revolutionary type of believer, but the bishops thought that, under control, they could be of great value. Not so the queen, who followed many particular orders with a general ban in 1576 for the whole of the Province of Canterbury. Grindal had been archbishop for less than a year, and his appointment had seemed the green light for evangelical Protestantism in England and a revival in the church. But Elizabeth was concerned with order, not revival, and insisted on repression. Grindal was not alone; a majority of the privy council – including men like William Cecil and Robert Dudley – were behind him, and so too many of his bishops. But this mass lobby was powerless against the queen's nose for potential trouble. Significantly there was one exception to the ban, the Province of York. There, aggressive Protestantism was a valuable corrective to Roman Catholic survival and revival; 'prophesyings' suited government objectives in the north, so 'prophesyings' remained.

By comparison with the 1576 situation, the position in Edward VI's reign looks more promising. The personal influence of the sovereign was in suspension and the influence of evangelical churchmen seems more considerable, with giants such as Cranmer, Ridley and Latimer. But this was not the contemporary assessment. Under Protector Somerset advance was made towards Protestantism, culminating in the first prayer book of 1549, but this did not please every reformer and it represented only what was felt safe against the pressures of foreign affairs and local un-rest. The reformers were divided amongst themselves, with Cranmer less influential than we may suppose. Erastianism, the subordination of church to state, was the keynote of policy. This remained true even when, under the Duke of Northumberland, Protestant advance accelerated under the stimulus of the more radical men the Duke favoured, unless he found them, like Knox 'ungrateful', that is, unwilling to part with church revenues! Friction among the reformers increased as Cranmer was up-braided for lack of 'zeal', and most serious of all, the pillage of church resources became blatant.

Thus, although the second prayer book in 1552 gave the church virtually its final theology and liturgy, there was little progress with the really significant problem – the revival of the church and the gospel. Indeed, the state showed positive discouragement of Cranmer's initiatives in this direction and the spoliation of church wealth put an effective limit to real reform. Thus frustration marched hand in hand with liturgical precocity.

In the state at large there were, it is true, a significant number of individuals who shared, in varying degrees, a Christian motiva-tion. But the influence which this had is problematic. Under the Protector Somerset a substantial campaign was launched for social justice and reform. However, the ideology behind it was largely traditional and the terms in which the government saw the problems were strongly influenced by its other preoccupations. For example, because it depended upon currency manipulation for any hope of paying its way, the state had to argue that enclosure of the open fields, not debasement of the coinage, was the main evil to be tackled. Certainly some social critics were close to Somerset's government, but they neither had exclusive in-fluence nor were all their notions equally acceptable.

There is, also, much to criticize in the approach of these enthusiasts, most of all their 'other-world' morality. The social

and economic problems of the mid-century were ascribed to sin
and greed, as no doubt – in Christian absolutes – they should have
been. But trying to cure unemployment by purging the country of
sin is hardly realistic. Hugh Latimer was a great preacher who
could work on his hearers to produce 'conscience-money', but
calling for repentance is not an effective way of bringing Christian
influence into the fabric of society. It is significant that the attack
on enclosures was led by an enthusiastic Protestant, John Hales, as
a crusade against 'covetousness'. The most effective diagnosis of
contemporary ills, on the other hand, was by Sir Thomas Smith
who rightly advocated reform of the coinage, and Smith was a
person lukewarm in religion.

The practical ineffectiveness of mid-century reformers contrasts
with the success of Thomas Cromwell a generation earlier. For too
long Cromwell has been blackened as an arch-politique and
hammer of religion, but it now seems clear that he was a convinced reformer, of moderate temper, no doubt, but none the less
genuine for that. He claimed that under his influence 'the Word of
God, the gospel of Christ, is not only favoured but also perfected,
set forth, maintained, increased and defended,' and we have no
reason to doubt his sincerity.[14] But what made Cromwell different
from the men of the 1540s and 1550s was that he was a man of
public affairs who knew how to get things done, and a man who,

unlike Grindal, accepted the self-evident truth that half a loaf is
better than no bread. If Grindal had bowed and lived to fight
another day, he would have done more for the gospel than he
achieved by pig-headed martyrdom. Cromwell certainly did.

The most important of Cromwell's successes was the printing
and dissemination of the English Bible, in defiance of a majority
of the English hierarchy. Cromwell had this interest in scripture
long before he met the translator Coverdale, and behind the
publication of the Bible in 1538 (in which Cromwell personally
lost £400) lies four years of preparatory effort by the minister. But
the Bible was not his only achievement. Cromwell's *Injunctions* of
1536 and 1538 were basic attempts to secure instruction in the
faith through preaching and catechising. He favoured reforming
preachers and writers. His attacks on superstition need no
reminder.

In all this Thomas Cranmer stood beside Cromwell, sharing the
same temper and the same attitudes. It was because of the
pragmatic, piecemeal reform which Cranmer had been preparing
under Henry VIII's patronage and veto that the advances under
Edward VI were possible at all. Would Cranmer have gained if he

had reacted like Grindal when Henry decided to defer the agreed attack on a number of superstitions? The King told his Archbishop to 'take patience herein, and forbear until we may espy a more apt and convenient time for that purpose,' and Cranmer obeyed.[15] Cranmer and Cromwell together laid the foundation of the Anglican church – moderate, erastian, biblical – and they did so without the emotion, the heroics and the defeats of the zealots.

Grindal, the Edwardian reformers, Cromwell and Cranmer: these were all Christians in or near government. What of Christian influence from the outside upon the policy of the state and the shaping of society? The great opportunity was presented by the existence and development of parliament as a forum where ideas could be promoted and pressure exerted.

Under Elizabeth and the early Stuarts there was a steady campaign for reform, with puritan enthusiasts in the van. The part of the campaign directed to further religious changes was a complete failure, as is well known. Less notice has been given to the programme for moral and social reform. Decency in clothing received attention in nine successive sessions of parliament, alcoholic drink in sixteen, sexual immorality was tackled in twelve bills, sabbath breaking and church attendance in sixteen, and so on. The case for reform was not presented in exclusively religious terms – the broader social problems of idleness, lack of education, public disorder and waste were always to the fore – and something was achieved in a few bills which reached the statute book, mainly in the 1620s.

Yet the total was small, given the effort, and this is explained by the considerable opposition aroused by bills to reform morals. What, in particular, was feared was interference with the lives of the gentry, and so too the threat of central interference through legislation in the jealously guarded preserves of the local magistrates. The men of property were quite prepared to use their powers in local government to regulate the behaviour of the lower classes as they thought necessary. They were unwilling to submit to a universal discipline imposed from the centre. Once again secular considerations triumphed.

The salt of the earth

There remains the influence of the gospel in its purely religious impact, as preaching and exhortation to the believer. The ineffectiveness of the general moral harangue is evident from the reign of Edward VI, but those were days when the authority of the preacher and the receptivity of the congregation were both in doubt. With the establishment of an effective puritan witness among important sections of both clergy and laity, the Elizabethan story was different. Reformed Catholicism was proscribed and tainted with treason; the Anglican establishment had yet to find a voice; the puritan message alone offered a Protestant answer to ordinary men concerned, not only with their souls but with the need to live good lives.

Thomas Fuller observed of the puritans, that what 'won them most repute was their ministers' painful preaching in populous places'. Missionary zeal was an enduring puritan trait, and Christopher Hill has shown the existence of an evangelical campaign to bring the gospel to 'the dark corners of the land'. William Wroth, the Welsh separatist cried: 'There are thousands of immortal souls around me, thronging to perdition; and should I not use all means to save them?' And this was not only zeal for 'souls', it implied an all-embracing serious morality, responsible to God and to one's neighbour, 'true happiness, both in this life and in the life to come':

> That they may be merry in the Lord, and yet without lightness; sad and heavy in heart for their own sins and the abominations of the land, and yet without discouragement or dumpishness.[16]

Ben Jonson's character, 'Zeal-of-the-Land Busy', was a recognizable puritan type, but so too and more so was Richard Greenham, the very influential puritan rector of Dry Drayton, near Cambridge, from 1570 to 1591. A staunch non-conformist and famous nation-wide as a spiritual adviser, he was prodigal in his efforts to relieve the poor and keep down food prices, even in 1586–87 organizing his own communal fund of cheap corn.

What this puritan way of life could achieve has been demonstrated by W.K.Jordan. The second half of the sixteenth century saw a major redistribution of charitable giving, which Jordan attributes directly to the reformers and especially the puritan divines. Now, instead of masses for the dead, the money provided hospitals, schools, almshouses – the very causes espoused by the puritan pamphleteers and preachers, and the very causes most of concern to the puritan congregations of city merchants and businessmen. In 1578 Thomas White challenged his London audience: 'What say you, [if] the poor lie in the streets in the time of the Gospel?'[17]

Faced with the waning of the traditional Catholic motives for charity, and with the inevitable reluctance to recognize that inflation requires inflated giving, puritan proclamation of the gospel inspired an ethic of charity which kept the level of voluntary giving abreast of biting inflation and channelled it into practical love for others. Henry, 'Silvertongued' Smith called on the Elizabethan parishioners of St Clement Danes to 'Give, give and give gladly...know that in the end what thou keepest thou shalt lose...'Ere you die, lay...forth for the profit of your poor brethren.'[18]

Drawing lessons from history is a perilous proposition. With the sixteenth and seventeenth centuries so remote from the present in assumptions and attitudes as well as in actual events, it is hard to reach conclusions which have any meaning today. But some warnings are clear. Dependence on the state fettered the church and prevented it acting as the body of Christ. Identification with society became so close as to distort the faith. Withdrawal from society offered no real escape for the believer. It was useless to offer spiritual remedies for material diseases – saving souls is not a practical way to act as 'the salt of the earth'. The revolutionary challenge to a community was less effective than the influence of committed Christians working within that community and organized group pressure was less productive than individual initiative. Christians made their biggest contribution to society when they acted as believers responding to the gospel.

That these conclusions are not necessarily all compatible and do not necessarily hold good at every point of the story tells us something about the nature of historical lessons and even more about the complexity of the relationship between the Christian and the community to which he belongs.

Notes and references

1 *Remains of Edmund Grindal*, ed. W.Nicholson, Parker Society, 1843, p. 387; the date is inferred from *ibid*. p.391.

2 *The King's Book*, ed. T.A.Lacey, SPCK, 1932, pp. 33–34, 36.

3 Nicholas Harpsfield, *Life and Death of Sir Thomas More*, ed. E.V.Hitchcock, Early English Text Society, 1932, p. 193.

4 John Whitgift, *Works*, ed. J.Ayre, Parker Society, 1851, i.21–22; *English Historical Documents*, v, 1485–1558 ed. C.H.Williams, Eyre and Spottiswoode, 1967, pp. 878, 876.

5 1 Peter 2:17; Proverbs 24:21 (Authorised Version).

6 Charles I, *Letters, Speeches and Proclamations*, ed. C.Petrie, Cassell, 1935, p. 200; S.R.Gardiner, *History of England, 1603–42*, Longmans, Green and Co., 1896, v.342.

7 R.C.Strong, *Portraits of Queen Elizabeth I*, Oxford University Press, 1963, p. 42.

8 *The Tudor Constitution*, ed. G.R.Elton, Cambridge University Press, 1960, p. 15.

9 D.H.Willson, *James VI and I*, Jonathan Cape, 1956, p. 207; *The Stuart Constitution* ed. J.P.Kenyon, Cambridge University Press, 1966, pp. 153–54; for this version of the epigram see Christopher Hill, *Puritanism and Revolution*, Secker and Warburg, 1958, p. 38 n.1.

10 C.H.Firth, 'The reign of Charles I', in *Transactions of the Royal Historical Society* 3rd series vi, 1912, 61.

11 P.Collinson, *The Elizabethan Puritan Movement*, Jonathan Cape, 1967, pp. 36, 45.

12 Anne Emily Newdigate-Newdegate, *Cavalier and Puritan*, Smith, Elder and Co., 1902, p. 198.

13 Henry Barowe, *Writings*, ed. L.H.Carlson, Allen and Unwin, 1962, i.84, 124–25, 188.

14 G.R.Elton, *Reform and Renewal*, Cambridge University Press, 1973, p. 34.

15 John Foxe, *Acts and Monuments*, Seeleys, 1858, v.562.

16 Thomas Fuller, *Church History of Britain*, Tegg and Son, 1837, iii. 101; Christopher Hill, 'Puritans and "the Dark Corners of the Land" ', in *Transactions of the Royal Historical Society*, 5th series 13 (1963), 98; Richard Rogers, *Seven Treaties* (1604), A5v.

17 W.K.Jordan, *Philanthropy in England 1480–1660*, Allen and Unwin, 1959, p. 169.

18 *ibid.* p. 167.

Chapter 12

The sword: war and violence in Europe, 1350–1650

'They have stuck to their livings and served Mars, the God of War, in the name of Christ, to the scandal of all religious mankind'.[1] So wrote George Bernard Shaw of the Christian clergy at the time of the 1914–18 War. The allegation is a common one. Among the most telling criticisms of Christianity is that at best it has been equivocal, at worst hypocritical in its attitude to violence. From the soldiers carrying the banner of the cross who waded up to the ankles in Muslim blood at the capture of Jerusalem in 1099, to the army chaplains of the twentieth century who promised that heaven awaited the man who died for king and country, the claim to be following Christ 'the Prince of Peace' appears a sick joke.

That the charge is in part true cannot be denied. Nevertheless we wrong the past if we forget that there is another side to the historical record. The problem of violence in society is complex, and that irrespective of religious presuppositions. It is hardly to be expected, then, that Christian solutions and responses are going to be simple.

Ethical attitudes towards coercion may be thought of as points on the compass, with four cardinal positions. The first is the belief that force is a legitimate and effective means to secure desired values. The second is the view that violence is inescapable in life and that it is necessary to come to terms with it. The third cardinal point is also to accept that violence exists, but to reject the idea of any accommodation. The final position argues that coercion is unnecessary, evil, and the obstacle which makes the good life impossible. We may describe these, respectively, as the positions of the crusader, the realist, the pacifist and the anarchist, and between them a mass of intermediate standpoints is possible.

This categorization is not specifically Christian, or even religious, but it applies most forcibly to Christianity in the later medieval and early modern history of Europe, the period roughly from the Black Death (1348–50) to the Thirty Years War (1618–48). During these three centuries European states began to develop something like effective permanent military resources, but at the same time they ostensibly recognized Christian assumptions and were subject to specific Christian advice and criticism. The framework of debate was acknowledged to be Christian and many people involved in making decisions on war and peace were Christians by particular commitment. Hence the exemplifications of the first three compass points are the 'Holy War', the 'Just War' and the 'Separated' or 'Gathered Church'. The fourth, the anarchist standpoint, was of less significance before the seventeenth century, but then it had clear, if partial, exposition in the radical writing of the English Revolution.

The background

To some extent, of course, the period under discussion in this chapter is too short. Christian attitudes to violence have a much older pedigree. In the first three centuries AD, Christians seem to have been unanimous in condemning 'the sword of war', and some even rejected 'the sword of justice', that is, the use of force in civilian police activity. Those who joined the army were expelled from the church and the refusal of Christians to help in the defence of society was part of the case against them. But such pacifism was relatively uncomplicated because few of these early believers were faced with the possibility of joining the Roman legions.

Towards the fourth century, however, matters began to change. Increasing numbers of Christians did join the army, more especially after the Emperor Constantine (312–337) officially recognized Christianity and his successors encouraged it. As K.S.Latourette remarked, 'in this victory of Christianity was also something of defeat', for with church and state now ranged together, belief had to come to terms with the compromises of power.[2] An early casualty was pacifism, ousted by classical notions of justifiable war. Athanasius (296–373) was the first Christian teacher to sanction killing in war, and Ambrose (340–397) rationalized the new situation with the argument that violence is a necessary function of love, since love commands the pursuit of justice. His even more influential disciple, Augustine (354–430) laid the basis of the realist Christian position in a careful theoretical discussion of the Just War.

A society dominated by the warrior

Accommodation of the faith to social reality also characterized the attitude of Christians to war in feudal society. The paradox of a community dominated by the warrior but also professing obedience to the teachings of Christ and his church was obscured by accepting as axiomatic the division of the community into those who fought, those who prayed and those who worked. As John Hale has pointed out, 'war itself was taken for granted, and the arguments for and against it hardly discussed.'³ Christian concern was with the regulation of violence – how and when force was justified – and the result was a careful analysis of the legal rights and wrongs of specific acts of aggression.

In the High Middle Ages the church used its power to enforce these regulations. Two devices, the 'Peace of God', dating from the late tenth century, and the 'Truce of God' from a little later, were attempts to establish non-combatant categories and neutral areas, and to limit the duration of fighting. The ideals of chivalry were seized on by the church to set before the warrior class the notion of the Christian knight, embodied in figures such as Parsifal or stories of the Round Table. The Council of Rheims (1119) tried to interdict religious ministrations in castles which received booty from unjust wars, and in 1139 the Second Lateran Council forbade jousts and tournaments. That much of this was ineffective is without question and it necessarily meant that the church tolerated war, but it did represent a genuine attempt from within the assumptions of a feudal community to insist that violence was subject to moral criteria.

At the end of the eleventh century, however, an opportunity seemed to be offered to make a more fundamental reconciliation between the warrior and the faith. This was the Crusade against the infidel. Instead of simply restricting, or endeavouring to restrict the warrior to what was 'just', Christian teaching could, in the Crusade, offer a sublimation of fighting in a holy war against the infidel, Muhammad. As with the ideals of chivalry, the crusading motives espoused by the church were by no means shared by all crusaders, but in religious terms, the Crusades were an appeal to force and to the duty of the fighting man, to bring God's will to pass. In calling for a crusade at the Council of Clermont in 1095, Pope Urban II said,

I beg and beseech you – and not I but Our Lord begs and beseeches you as heralds of Christ – rich and poor alike, make haste to drive this evil from the places where our brothers live and bring a very present help to the worshippers of Christ...If anyone who sets out should lose his life...his sins shall be par-

doned from that moment...May those men who have been occupied in the wicked struggle of private warfare against their
fellow Christians now take up arms against the infidel and help
to bring this long-delayed campaign to a victorious end. May
those who have been brigands now become soldiers and those
who have fought against their own families now fight as they
should against barbarians. Let those who have served for
mercenaries' pay now earn an everlasting reward and let those
who have dissipated their body and soul now gather their
strength to win a double prize.[4]

The fullest embodiment of this militant Christianity was the
military order, the Templars, the Hospitallers and the rest. Made
up of men who took monastic vows, they devoted themselves to
the military life and to war against the infidel; indeed, they were
prohibited from fighting against Christians. Here is the ideal of
the warrior dedicated to the service of God and the extension of
his kingdom. The individual who personified this rapprochement
between the word and the sword was St Louis, Louis IX of France.
An earnest Christian who used his journeys as an opportunity to
pray, renowned for his simple morality, Louis saw his public office
as the divine call which had kept him out of the religious life. At
home he suppressed private war, the carrying of arms and private
vengeance, yet he was personally the mirror of chivalry and twice a
crusader, indeed, he died as one.

But the reconciliation of the church and the warrior was abor-
tive because the crusading ideal became debased. The perverting
of the Fourth Crusade, (1202–4) into an attack on Constantinople
incurred the wrath of Pope Innocent III, but he was not averse to
an attempt to profit by the destruction of the Byzantine church. In
1208 he went further and preached a crusade of his own against
the allegedly Manichaean heretics in the south of France. In what
was the rape of Languedoc by the barons of the north, the Papal
Legate was, it is said, asked about the dangers of killing Catholics
along with heretics. Fearful of heretics masquerading as true sons
of the church he replied, 'Slay them all, God will know his own.'[5]
From this moment on, the Crusade became merely one of the
standard temporal weapons in the armoury of the Holy See.

As the defence of war as a possibly holy calling rang more and
more hollow, Christians were left with the Just War hypothesis and
nothing more. Only outside orthodox religion was there any hint
of the third possibility, withdrawal from the contaminated world.
Refusal to shed blood was one of the axioms of the Waldensians

who appeared in the later twelfth century and flourished until the seventeenth, and is found among other heretics too. But as John Hale has said, the stream of pacifist argument is a thin one.

The Just War

Turning now to the period between the Black Death and the Thirty Years War, we have first to observe the fortunes of the Just War. Viewed from a practical standpoint, the Just War concept became fatuous. The more it was refined, the more untenable it became. 'The problem of war and peace in the Middle Ages', J.H.Hexter has written, 'enmeshed Western men in ethical dilemmas, paradoxes and contradictions which were bound to strain the considerable proficiency of moralists in the arts of self-deception, obfuscation and weaseling.[6]

A study of the Anglo-French wars of the fourteenth century has shown that the poet John Gower, while no pacifist, swung away from his earlier acceptance that Edward III's claim to France was just. In particular the involvement of the church in violence disgusted him: 'Peter preached, but today the church fights.'[7] Increasingly it became possible to claim that almost any recourse to violence was justified. By the end of the sixteenth century a government could go to war to defend lands, faith, goods or liberty, in reprisal for acts of piracy, to avenge insults to its ambassadors, to defend friends and allies, to enforce treaties and to deny reinforcements to an enemy; allies could be assisted and a preventative campaign could be just – the pre-emptive strike. The early seventeenth century added war which was probably but not demonstrably just, and war when a prince considered that his country's essential supplies were endangered.

For the English, as we have seen, divine approval for state violence became a point of faith. The thirty-seventh of the *Thirty-Nine Articles* declares:

> The Laws of the Realm may punish Christian men with death for heinous and grievous offences...It is lawful for Christian men, at the commandment of the Magistrate to wear weapons and serve in the wars.

As an effective check upon violence, Christian categories of just and unjust wars ceased to have any importance.

But it would be wrong to suppose that there was no honest re-examination of the Just-War hypothesis by Christians of this period, especially among Roman-Catholic jurists. The Dutch pope, Adrian VI (1459–1523), argued that a prince's subjects who are in doubt about the justice of a war must refuse to serve in it. Mazzolini (1460–1523), a contemporary Italian jurist, sought to limit the scope of reprisals. Cajetan, the Italian cardinal who demanded Luther's surrender in 1518 at an imperial Diet at Augsburg, did allow the Just War to include aiding allies, but he was resolute in the view that without a wrong suffered no war could ever be just.

The chief occasion for Christian protest against an unjust war arose from the conquest by the Spaniards of Central and South America. In 1511, the Dominican Antonio de Montesinos preached a startling sermon to the settlers on Hispaniola in which he asked: 'On what authority have you waged a detestable war against these people who dwelt quietly and peacefully on their own land?', and from then on the protest grew. Bartolomé de las Casas, a settler himself, became converted to this view, entered the Dominican order, and for fifty years clamoured in support of his Indians. For him the claim that Spain's rule in America was made legitimate by her superiority in arms (which was in fact the position), was 'an absurd, nefarious argument, unworthy of being advanced by Christian and reasonable men'.[8]

The most notable examination of war in the context of European expansion was in a series of lectures delivered in the 1530s by one of de las Casas' fellow Dominicans, Francisco de Vitoria (d. 1546), professor of theology at Salamanca. He justified Spanish occupation according to what we would now describe as the fundamental principles of international law, indeed, we can say that international law developed from the Just War theory. But before this came a bitter demolition of the usual arguments permitting violence.

Was war justified as a means of forcing unbelievers to accept the faith? – no; in order to prevent their sinning? – no. Even though self-defence by the Spaniards would be just, yet the Spaniards should use minimum force because the Indians were innocent and justified in being frightened of the strangers. Should the Indians attack after they knew the real situation, Spain must make only a limited reply. In strict conformity with Augustine, Vitoria insisted that not only must a just war arise from a wrong done, but it must lead to a just result – peace and safety – and be waged with due proportion. Even when war was justified – and this was only in cases where, had a court been available, a successful prosecution of the wrongdoer would have been possible – it might not be wise. Force was justified where facilities for preaching the gospel were refused, since this was for the further good of the pagan, but the text 'all things are lawful to me but all things are not expedient' must be borne in mind. De Vitoria ends with a statement of the three canons of warfare.

1. Assuming that a prince has authority to make war, he should first of all not go seeking occasions and causes of war, but should, if possible, live in peace with all men, as St Paul enjoins on us. Moreover he should reflect that others are his neighbours, whom we are bound to love as ourselves, and that we all have one common Lord, before whose tribunal we shall have to render our account. For it is the extreme of savagery to seek for and rejoice in grounds for killing and destroying men whom God has created and for whom Christ died. But only under compulsion and reluctantly should he come to the necessity of war.

2. When war for a just cause has broken out, it must not be waged so as to ruin the people against whom it is directed, but only so as to obtain one's rights and the defence of one's country and in order that from that war, peace and security may in time result.

3. When victory has been won and the war is over, the victory should be utilized with moderation and Christian humility, and the victor ought to deem that he is sitting as judge between two States, the one which has been wronged and the one which has done the wrong, so that it will be as judge and not as accuser that he will deliver the judgement whereby the injured State can obtain satisfaction and this, so far as possible, should involve the offending State in the least degree of calamity and misfortune, the offending individuals being chastised within lawful limits; and an especial reason for this is that in general among Christians all the fault is to be laid at the door of their princes, for subjects when fighting for their princes act in good faith and it is thoroughly unjust that for every folly their kings commit, the punishment should fall upon their subjects.[9]

It is hardly surprising that both pope and emperor should have been incensed by an academic who challenged their morality and their titles, and did so publicly and by name. Charles V ordered an enquiry and forbade any further treatment of the subject; when the lectures were published in 1557, the Vatican took action to place them on the Index, but the pope died first. It may be that the Just War degenerated in practice to a tatty propaganda device, but nobody can deny that Christians such as de las Casas or de Vitoria were devoutly attempting to answer the question, 'What is the mind of Christ?'

In practical terms, of course, the Christian attack on the Conquistadores was ineffective until too late to help most of their victims. It stood little chance against men who roundly rejected the idea of a missionary campaign. Francisco Pizarro said, 'I have not come for any such reasons. I have come to take away from them their gold.'[10] In Europe itself the careful calculation of just and unjust stood even less chance with the coming of religious controversy which, instead, breathed new life into the discredited hypothesis of the Holy War – not now for the papacy, but for God's truth.

The Holy War

The call for a Holy War could come from the radical position of the person who wished to usher in the Kingdom, as well as from conservatives repeating, under new circumstances and with a new fervour, the gospel of the Crusade against the heretic. The European tradition of the suppression of heresy by violent means, whether individual persecution or mass repression, the identification of church and state which made religious dissent into rebellion, and a plentiful supply of metaphor, simile and analogy in scripture suggesting the physical resistance of evil by the godly, all this combined to produce the blasphemy of the religious wars.

Thomas Muntzer, a colleague of Martin Luther, but independently under the influence of German mysticism and imbued with the apocalyptic vision, believed that the sword had a definite role in God's plan. The classic biblical authority is chapter thirteen of Paul's letter to the Romans:

> For government, a terror to crime, has no terrors for good behaviour. You wish to have no fear of the authorities? Then continue to do right and you will have their approval, for they are God's agents working for your good. But if you are doing wrong, then you will have cause to fear them; it is not for nothing that they hold the power of the sword, for they are God's agents of punishment, for retribution on the offender.

For Muntzer this is not restricted to law and order. It is an instruction to use the sword to destroy the godless and Anti Christ. The princes are the primary servants of the sword, but if they fail 'the sword will be taken from the princes and given to the zealous common people', and the purpose is 'the destruction of the godless'.

The corollary of this is the right to resist the tyrant, who is defined as a ruler who usurps God's authority by repressing the godly. 'If anyone wants to fight the Turk, he need not go far; the Turk is in the land.' The tyrant may chasten only for a short time; power is to be taken by the common people and the persecutors 'must be strangled like dogs'. Non-resistance is a surrender to godlessness, earning pretty songs about martyrdom and 'the villainy of the godless would never rightly come into its own.[11]

Muntzer made no distinction between the law of the Old Testament and the law of Christ; the New Testament ethic is absorbed into an Old Testament context. The sword prepared the way for salvation, and that meant the destruction of all who caused the godly to stumble – hence all who were comprised in the church-state power structure. The result was the gospel of a revolutionary crusade to 'pull down the mighty from their seats':

> You must root out the weeds from the vineyard of the Lord in time of the harvest. Then the beautiful red grain will win firm roots and shoot up rightly. But the angels who sharpen their sickles for this task are the serious servants of God who fulfil the zeal of divine wisdom.[12]

Turned on its head, the same attitude justified the national churches in their military zeal, with the ultimate perversion of 'God on our side'. Whatever the denomination, the clergy can be found proclaiming from the pulpit the godliness of slaughter as the prince desired. The pulpits of Paris rang with the call to cleanse the land of the Huguenot. Change the names and you get the situation in London. James Bisse, Fellow of Magdalen College, Oxford, said in a sermon of 1581:

> By Elizabeth, a Woman, the goats of Italy, the Wolves of Spain, the Cormorants of Rome, the Irish colts and the foxes of England that are now in Ireland and all other he enemies shall be brought to shame....Go tell them...that those goats, Wolves, Cormorants, Colts, Foxes shall be so hunted and baited by an English Grey, that no one of them shall be left to piss against a wall.[13]

The Huguenot battle hymn was the metrical version of Psalm 118, 'This is the day the Lord hath made, we will rejoice and be glad in it'. They sang it in the saddle at Coutras, and then smashed the royalist army, leaving 3,400 dead. At Dunbar, Cromwell's cavalry were pressed for time, so they sang Psalm 117, the shortest in the book. When the Spanish Armada left Lisbon, every man went first to confession and took communion; the pope granted absolution and indulgence to those taking part, and the banner of the expedition had on it the arms of Spain in between the Crucifix and the Blessed Virgin Mary. The English and Dutch, not to be outdone, attributed victory to God – 'God blew with his winds, and they were scattered'.

Humanist opposition to war

We have so far followed the fortunes of two of the four classic positions which Christians have adopted towards war, violence in the service of God and violence as something which can be subjected to God's control. The third position sees violence as a thing to be shunned, but before considering this, we need to look at a powerful school of thought which is almost, but not quite, in this pacifist position – a bare degree away from the cardinal point, but with still a slight tendency to swing back to realism. This is the school which we know as Christian Humanists or the Erasmian reformers.

Erasmus of Rotterdam (1466–1536) was unquestionably the scholar of his age, with a European predominance which has hardly been equalled. In religion, Erasmus, as is well known, proclaimed a simple imitation of the life of Christ inspired by the practice of prayer and straightforward Bible study. For Erasmus nothing was more fundamental to this 'philosophy of Christ' than hostility to war. It is found in what he wrote in his early days as a monk and in his latest productions. The comments in his collection of proverbs, *The Adages*, are mostly brief, except for the gloss on 'War is pleasant to those who have not tried it'. Over the years this grew to a long and bitter essay on the subject. *The Complaint of Peace* (1517) offers a complete tract, full of power and passion:

> What is the prayer of the soldier during the service [before a battle]?
>
> 'Our Father' – how can you dare to call Him 'Father' as you go forth to slay your brother?
>
> 'Hallowed be Thy name' – How could the name of God be more dishonoured than by your fighting?
>
> 'Thy kingdom come' – Are you praying that so much shedding of blood aid tyranny?
>
> 'Thy will be done on earth as it is in heaven' – His will is to preserve the peace and you prepare for war.
>
> You ask for daily bread from your Father and at the same time you destroy the crops of your brother and hope their destruction will hasten his death. How can you repeat 'and

forgive us our trespasses as we forgive those who trespass against us' when you rush out to slay your brother? With danger to yourself and your neighbour you ask to avoid the dangers of temptation. You ask deliverance from evil and yet at the instigation of the Evil One you prepare evil for your brother.[14]

This was not all. Erasmus attempted to use his influence with the crowned heads of Europe to secure peace. His tract *On the Christian Prince* was intended to instruct the young Charles of Habsburg:

> While other things have their attending evils, war is the shipwreck of all that is good in a sea of iniquity. No calamity prolongs itself with more tenacity – war springs from war, the greatest from the least, two wars from one, fierce and bloody war from a tourney; and the plague rising in one place spreads its infection to the neighbouring peoples, nay to the most remote.[15]

To readers of English, the attack on war in Thomas More's *Utopia* is probably better known than the work of Erasmus. The loathing of the Utopian community for violence provides an implied comparison with the reality of Europe in 1517, but More goes much further than this. He mounts an assault upon the soldiers and aristocrats of Europe, what Hexter calls 'a blanket condemnation of a very large section of Europe's power elite'. His friend Dean Colet preached before Henry VIII that wars were seldom undertaken except from hatred and ambition, and that the model for the Christian ruler should be Christ, not Caesar or Alexander. Christian humanists everywhere agreed with Erasmus, 'Whoever brings tidings of Christ brings tidings of peace. Whoever proclaims war proclaims him who is most unlike Christ.'[16]

It was, moreover, not simply a matter of preaching. The true Christian humanist sought to serve his prince as a wise counsellor, and it has been argued that the influence of such thinking can be seen in England in the policies of Thomas Wolsey. Certainly he gave practical reasons for disliking war – notably the expense, but his frequent praise of peace seems to have been genuine enough to earn commendation from Erasmus and bring hope to More. Wolsey's predecessor as chancellor, Archbishop Warham, also earned praise from Erasmus for his work for peace:

> Would that all our princes were the same mind that is in you. Then these insane and wretched wars would end and rulers

would turn their minds to making their age illustrious by the arts of peace.[17]

But although such deeply felt commitment must be applauded, the school of Christian Humanists was, perhaps, too intelligent and sophisticated. Ardent in condemning war, it never completely advocated withdrawal from all contact with or support for violence. Erasmus could still write for the future Charles V, 'the good and Christian prince should regard every war, however just, as a thing suspect.'[18] But suspect is one thing, forbidden another and, after a life of war, the emperor was to die claiming, perhaps justly, that he had never been guilty of aggression.

The humanists were in a cleft stick. The Erasmian ideal was of a world remade by a Christocentric ethical piety spreading from the wise councillor to the prince and so to the people. Out-and-out pacifism which disqualified the councillor from serious attention would, therefore, have been self-defeating, a point made with wit and passion in *Utopia*; Colet had to explain away his sermon to Henry VIII by saying that he was only attacking unjust wars. Further, Erasmus saw the office of the ruler as specifically Christian, a place in which to serve Christ. Recognized authority had the obligation to establish justice, thus judge and executioner were not in the same case as the warrior. At a deeper level, too, prohibition was contrary to Erasmus' emphasis on personal response to and deliberate imitation of Christ as the necessary dynamic of Christian living.

> If the whole doctrine of Christ is not everywhere opposed to war, if one instance can be cited where it is commended, then let us Christians fight...Even against the Turks I think we should not go thoughtlessly to war...First let us see to it that we are truly Christian, and then, if it seems good, attack the Turks.[19]

In a sense, therefore, Christian Humanism while pacific was not pacifist, because pacifism is a thing of law and peaceableness a thing of grace.

The pacifist case

The note of unreserved pacifism, the refusal to take part in either collective violence or judicial violence springs out of the Hussite reformation in fifteenth-century Bohemia, in the writing of Peter Chelchitzky.

 Almost unheard of outside Czechoslovakia because of his use of the vernacular, Chelchitzky, within the last twenty years, has been recognized as one of the great Christian thinkers of Europe. Very little is known about him. He was probably born in about 1390 in a small village 210 km/130 miles south of Prague, but nothing certain is known of his social position or education. Although under some Waldensian influence, he was swept up in the Hussite movement, the Czech revolt against the Holy Roman Emperor which began in 1419. He belonged to the socially radical wing, the Taborites, but to a minority within them which retained the initial Taborite views on non-resistance and rejected the later military revolution led by Jan Ziska. He spent most of his life at his home village, with a group of disciples, and from 1421 produced a series of vernacular writings of the first importance. The first three set out his position. One argued that the Christian warfare is spiritual, not material; another claimed that the state was unchristian; the third attacked the medieval division of society into three estates. Chelchitzky died in the 1460s, but his influence was crucial in the founding of the Bohemian Brethren.

John Wycliffe, the inspiration of Jan Hus, had allowed the use of force in the expulsion of evil if spiritual weapons were not sufficient, and Hus had permitted war 'in defence of faith and truth', but Chelchitzky rejected their views. Temporal force and Christ's way of love are, for him, irreconcilable; the conversion of Constantine was a disaster for the faith. Authority must be cruel or perish; it cannot, therefore, be loving. The state must be totally rejected and Christ's law of love put in its place. He will have nothing to do with Christian rule to reform bad Christians or unbelievers – conversion comes through the workings of the law of God, that is loving God and your neighbour. If a Christian ruled by force he would sin. Reform is impossible – power can be wielded only 'by the worst of men who are without any faith or virtue, since it is by means of terrible punishments that the state compels evildoers to some measure of justice in outward matters'.[20] He rejected any implication in Romans 13 of participation by Christians in the state; he saw there nothing beyond submission. Non-resistance was the only allowable response to persecution.

Chelchitzky accepted that for the sake of non-Christians and false-Christians the state must exist, and the Christian must render unto Caesar his due. But the Christian has no part in the state and the state has no part in the church. No Christian can be a ruler. The death penalty is totally incompatible with the injunction, 'love your enemies'. 'The executioner who kills is as much a wrongdoer as the criminal who is killed.' As for the Old Testament toleration of war, he ascribed this to the lower standards of pre-Christian times. Under Christ all men were brothers, and that was what mattered, whatever the doctors of the church had said about the possibility of a Just War. 'If St Peter himself should suddenly appear from Heaven and begin to advocate the sword and to gather together an army in order to defend the truth and establish God's order by worldly might, even then I would not believe him.'[21]

Chelchitzky's views did not survive for long. The military pressures of late fifteenth-century Bohemia and the gradual entry into the Brethren of social groups which expected to take part in government brought about a schism. The 'Minor Party', those adhering to Chelchitzky's vision, struggled on until the mid-sixteenth century, but the victorious 'Major Party' abandoned many of his ideals. By about 1500, Brethren were being admonished to avoid participation in war, though categories of 'just' and 'unjust' wars are defined vaguely with the advice that one is more tolerable than the other. They were advised to hire a substitute where possible or where not, to try for non-combatant duties. Failing that, they were to

> avoid pushing themselves forward as well as the acquisition of glory through bravery, since excessive bravery as well as cruelty and looting and booty and avaricious desires and other unrighteousness were to be shunned. They were not to proceed willingly to these things [war service] but only under compulsion with the wish to be free of them. They were to beseech God to deliver them from evil, for in war many evils come to pass.

Killing in war is still seen as murder, but the guilt rests primarily on the instigator who has no just cause, and least of all on those 'who being under compulsion cannot escape, yet have no thought of murder...nor of any unrighteousness'.[22]

The banner of pacifism passed in the sixteenth century to the Anabaptists – a term whose definition always causes problems, but which can, for these purposes, be regarded as the contemporary label for Protestants who were more radical than the major groupings of Luther, Zwingli and Calvin. They were never a single organized sect and they differed considerably amongst themselves, but from the 1560s onwards, whatever else they did not share, they shared the belief in a-political pacifism, with a reasoning akin to that of Chelchitzky.

This had been from an early date the position of the Swiss Anabaptists, although initially there had been tension between the gospel of peace and using the sword to bring in the Kingdom. The

Schleitheim Confession of 1527 sets out this Swiss consensus. It eschewed

> all popish and anti-popish works and Church services, meetings and church attendance, drinking-houses, civic affairs, the commitments made in unbelief and other things of that kind...Therefore there will also unquestionably fall from us the unchristian, devilish weapons of force – such as sword, armour and the like and all their use.[23]

The sword belonged to the magistrate for use against evil-doers; it was wrong for Christians to use it, even in self-defence, and they had to take no part in government or in litigation. In the period before this position became generally accepted there were considerable local variations, one of which produced the tragedy of Munster in 1534 and the practice of terrorism which continued to occur for some years. Gradually, however, the Schleitheim Confession won through; in contrast to the Bohemian Brethren, it was separation which triumphed.

There is little sign among the Anabaptists of any anarchist element, arguing for no use of force at all. Obedience must be required in the secular area. Coercion, however, functions only for fallen mankind and there is no role for the Christian as magistrate or ruler. A confession of 1539 answered the question whether a Christian can assume government office if elected with the following:

> Christ was to be made a king, but He fled, not seeking the ordinance of His Father. We do likewise and follow Him, for then we shall not walk in darkness. 'The Kingdom of Christ is not of this world'. He also says, 'Whoever will follow me must deny himself, take up his cross and follow me.' He himself forbade the power of the sword and said, 'The princes of this world rule the nations and the overlords employ force, but this is not how it should be with you.'

Pacifism was an issue on which disobedience to the state was mandatory. Wolfgang Brandhuber wrote in 1529 to the believers at Rattenberg:

> In the matter of war, take care that you do not make the mistake of defending your body, as if you were going to be obedient to the government in this matter, for this is always contrary to God. However, in all else which is not contrary to God with respect to person and property, one should be obedient to the government.[24]

Withdrawal from the world and its evil gave the Anabaptists a coherent and simple attitude to violence which is attractive against the moral contortions of Christians who admitted the possibility of recourse to force. But it brings up again the fundamental illogicality of the Anabaptist ideal: it depended upon the existence and energy of the very state it spurned. In particular, the problem of taking a share in the general guard and police duties of a community was never resolved. The majority tradition of Mennonite Anabaptists was able to secure exemption from liability to such duties in the states of Holland and Zealand, but in the other provinces of the United Netherlands, military obligations were redeemed by a poll tax. As J.W.Allen pointed out many years ago, 'to pay the poll-tax was to pay others to kill, and be killed, for them.' It was the equivalent to accepting coercion! In order to survive, the Mennonites had compromised the Schleitheim position. The most belligerent of modern English kings, William III, certainly found them no incubus, and no witness to the truth either.

> I have always been assured of the submissive and peaceful spirit of the Mennonites, who behave themselves with resignation and perfect obedience towards their superiors, leading a peaceful and laborious life and contributing willingly to the upkeep of the State and of the country in which they live, to which they render themselves useful by their industry and their work.[25]

The Reformers: Luther

What of the major reformers? As is well known, neither Luther, Zwingli nor Calvin rejected the sword. Indeed, each has episodes in his career which apologists would prefer to forget – Luther's hysterical plea for slaughter of the peasants, Zwingli's death in battle and Calvin's pursuit of Servetus. Luther remained in the realist position which by tradition had taken the form of the Just War hypothesis, but his argument was somewhat different.

Medieval political thought, as we have seen, had made much use of the text in Luke ' "Look, Lord," they said, "we have two swords here." "Enough, enough", he replied.' This was a basis for a dual theory of authority, one sword for temporal power and one for spiritual power. Luther, however, based his ideas on Romans 13 which speaks of a single sword which belongs to the state. Political authority, said Luther, was God's instrument to punish evil and protect the good; coercion was necessary to prevent anarchy.

We must briskly and confidently let the Sword cut into the law-breakers as St Paul teaches in Romans 13. Let no one think that the world will be ruled without blood. The worldly sword shall and must be red and bloody, because the world will and must be bad.

What would happen, he asks, if a shepherd put wolves, lions, eagles and sheep together and told them to be good.[26]

How did this relate to Christianity? In a sense it did not, because, as Luther pointed out, 'Christians among themselves need no law or sword'. Nevertheless, the use of force belongs to God and is part of the principle of political authority which he built into the world at creation.

God has established two kinds of government among men: the one is spiritual: it has no sword but it has the Word [of God] by which men...may attain everlasting life. The other is worldly government through the sword which aims to keep peace among men and this he rewards with temporal blessing.

Thus it is nonsense to think of achieving Christian objectives by government; the sword has an ethically negative effect in preventing the growth of evil, but it makes no contribution to the triumph of good:

Such order we must have, but it is not a way to get to heaven, and the world will not be saved because of it, but it is necessary exactly to keep the world from getting worse.[27]

On the other hand, it is an error to say that Luther abandons the world to the devil. In the first place, civil government is 'a glorious ordinance of God and a splendid gift of God'; it is part of God's general care for the creation; its values are those of God – 'God is the founder of both kinds of righteousness', Christian and civil. In the second place, the Christian can properly and rightly take up public service as a service to God; they should volunteer, Luther tells us, if there is a shortage of 'hangmen, police, judges, lords or princes':

But you ask whether the policeman, hangmen, lawyers, counsel and the like can also be Christians and in a state of salvation...I answer: if the state and its sword are a divine service...then that which the state needs to wield the sword must also be a divine service.

And it is not a service in which the Christian suspends his Christianity. A Christian serves God in and through his vocation and Luther instructs the Christian ruler on the way his Christianity should inform his rule. Like Christ he should empty himself of all self-regard and rule in love, but always recognizing that love is not leniency. His example should be the biblical rulers who 'have wielded the Sword sternly in their office and strangled people like chickens, and are nevertheless tender, mild and friendly in their hearts'.[28]

The Anabaptist retort was that this plainly contradicted the gospel! Christ and the apostles forbade the use of force and enjoined non-resistance by specific injunction and by example. To this Luther replied that for an individual believer to renounce the use of force in his own defence was one thing; the use of force to check wickedness in the community interest was quite different. Love commands its use, for 'love of neighbour seeks not its own, how great or small, but considers how profitable and needful for neighbour and community such works are'. It was precisely their challenge to the duty of the Christian to support the divine ordinance of government which led Luther to condemn the radicals and ultimately to sanction the death penalty for Anabaptists. A memorandum of 1531, written by Luther's colleague Melanchthon but signed by Luther, stated:

> They [the Anabaptists] teach that a Christian should not use a sword, should not serve as a magistrate, should not swear or hold property, may desert an unbelieving wife. These articles are seditious and the holders of them may be punished with the sword. We must pay no attention to their avowal 'we did no one any harm', because if they persuaded everybody there would be no government.[29]

The Reformers: Zwingli

If Luther represents a variety of the realist position which justifies righteous violence in the service of order, Zwingli represents a realist flirting with the activist, crusading concept. His stress was that 'the Kingdom of Christ is also external'.[30] Therefore the Christian does not simply wait for some eschatological consummation; erecting the Kingdom is a legitimate goal for the individual believer and the believing community. Here is the community politics of Zurich speaking. There is, however, a deep theological foundation as well. Because there is one supreme God no values can be outside his domain. The highest and best polity must equal the Kingdom of God, and it must be possible to serve God through politics.

The consequence of this insight was that Zwingli was ambivalent and fluctuating on the subject of violence. The early Zwingli treats us to partisan Swiss patriotism – opposed to the trade in mercenaries (a traditional view of the comparatively affluent Zurich) but prepared to accept a just papal war. Under the impact of the Swiss defeat at Marignano in 1515 and the reading of Erasmus, Zwingli veered to the position that patriotic defence was allowed, but not war.

> Each one should consider war's danger to him if he would be treated as he treats other Christians. A foreign mercenary violently invades your country, devastates your meadows, fields and vineyards, drives off your cattle, gathers up your belongings and carries them off. He has previously slain your sons in the attack as they defended themselves and you, raped and disgraced your daughters, and kicked away your dear wife as she fell at his feet, begging mercy for her and you. And he drags you forth, good old man, hiding fearfully in your own house and miserably slays you in the presence of your wife, despite your trembling advanced age and the misery and sorrow of your good wife; and last of all, he burns house and farm. You think that, if the heavens did not open and spit out fire and the earth tear apart and swallow up such a villain, there would be no God. But if you do the same to someone else, you say it is the law of war![31]

An erstwhile mercenary chaplain, Zwingli knew what he was talking about. But as the tensions within the Swiss Confederation and the pressure of the reformers drove the Catholic cantons to ally with the Habsburgs, Zwingli swung again, returning to the justification of war in defence of God's peace. Everything became relative to the progress of the gospel and the glory of Zurich, which was the same thing.

Like Luther, Zwingli accepted that there was only one sword of authority and that its purpose was to protect the good and punish the wicked, to ensure that the 'human community does not become a community of murder'. But for Zwingli there was not the distinction which Luther made between the principles of creation and the principles of the Kingdom of Christ; the laws of nature, of Moses and of Christ were a continuum and a hierarchy, with the first two providing the basis for the third. Thus, the use of the sword according to the law of nature could serve Christ. Further, since the law of Christ could never be totally realized in this life, the role of human law is to strive towards the ideal. Hence there is a need to progress and it is small wonder that Zwingli believed that 'a church without the magistrate is mutilated and incomplete'.[32]

Of course Zwingli never believed that the Kingdom of God was solely a matter of the community and he did not expect that it could or would reach an advanced stage in any particular state. His insistence, rather, was positive. Even though it would be less than perfect, a Christian community must be part of any real understanding of the Christian gospel; it is the standard. For the Christian ruler,

> all his laws are similar to the will of God, not exactly similar, but having something of the image of the divine law and will; for the justice at which the judge must arrive is only a shadow of true justice.[33]

It is, therefore, unfair to condemn Zwingli's last years of military preparation and diplomatic manoeuvring as time-serving. He knew he could not bring in the Kingdom by force, but he believed that force in proper circumstances could help to bring in 'something of the image of the divine law'. There is neither remorse nor hypocrisy in his last recorded words before he left Zurich to fight and die at the battle of Cappel, 'keep faith with our Lord Christ and his church'.[34]

The Reformers: Calvin

With John Calvin the picture of a compass to illustrate ethical attitudes to violence begins to fail. At one and the same time he seems to be of the realist school and a crusader. Like Luther he derived the state and its rights from the will of God:

> It comes not of the perversity of man that kings and other lords have power upon earth, but it comes of the providence and holy ordinance of God, whom it has pleased to manage in this fashion the government of man.

In consequence, rulers are

> the ordained guardians and vindicators of public innocence, modesty, honour and tranquillity, so that it should be their only study to provide for the common peace and safety...But as rulers cannot do this unless they protect the good against the injuries of the bad, and give aid and protection to the oppressed, they are armed with power to curb manifest evildoers and criminals, by whose misconduct the public tranquillity is disturbed or harassed.

Christ's commands not to kill are quite separate from this; the magistrate 'acts not of himself, but executes the very judgements of God', indeed,

> to sheath the sword and keep their hands pure from blood, while nefarious men wade through murder and slaughter, so far from redounding to the praise of their goodness and justice, would be to incur the guilt of the greatest impiety.

The justification for the sword of war is an extension of this justification for the sword of justice: the robber and the invader are two examples of the same case. Certainly Calvin only allows the defensive war and he warns against 'private feeling', but within these limits his conviction is firm: war is lawful.[35]

Thus far Calvin is a realist, but there is also the Calvin who seems to hint at a more positive role for violence. The starting point is his vigorous statement of the duty of non-resistance to authority, something which he shared with Luther. Even the most tyrannical of rulers must be obeyed and, says Calvin, obeyed with reverence because 'the obedience which [subjects] yield is rendered to God himself, insomuch as the power [of princes and governors] is from God'.[36] The only qualification is the prior duty to obey express commands from God, but if this conflicts with the command of the ruler then the Christian has patiently to accept his ruler's wrath; he is never to resist.

Calvin, however, is well aware of the paradox of 'an impious king' who was, nevertheless a 'minister of God'. He tries to meet it in a number of ways, two of particular interest. God, he argues, does punish the evil king, sometimes by foreign invasion but sometimes by raising up 'manifest avengers from among his own servants', 'deliverers brought forward by the lawful call of God'. Secondly Calvin points to political systems which include subordinate magistrates, representative machinery or provisions for consultation. The status of such individuals and institutions is not delegated from the sovereign but is derived from God. It follows from this that

> if they connive at kings when they tyrannize and insult over the humbler of the people, I affirm that their dissimulation is not free from nefarious perfidy, because they fraudulently betray the liberty of the people, while knowing that, by the ordinance of God, they are its appointed guardians.

Certainly the loop-hole in absolute non-resistance does not appear large, and in 1561 Calvin interpreted it to the French

Huguenots in a restricted sense, but the potential scope for violence had been admitted: it was now possible to justify both tyrannicide and organized rebellion.[37]

Force also became more significant in the Calvinist scheme as Geneva began to play a large diplomatic role in defence of Protestantism. Calvin could now toy with a French alliance which might produce European conflict and write:

> We might ascribe it more to a blameworthy sense of security than to genuine trust in God, if we were to ignore means of assistance which, even though not desirable, are still permitted.

Another factor was the challenge of heresy. Calvin's *Institutes* proclaim that the first duty of the magistrate is to foster true religion. Under threat from heterodox critics such as Michael Servetus and the arguments of Sebastian Castelion, this was spelled out as the right of the magistrate to enforce orthodoxy by the death penalty if need be:

> Whoever shall maintain that wrong is done to heretics and blasphemers in punishing them, makes himself an accomplice in their crime and guilty as they are. There is no question here of man's authority: it is God who speaks and clear is it what law he will have kept in the Church even to the end of the world.[38]

This crusading tendency in Calvinism is even more clearly seen in the leader on whom the mantle of Calvin fell, Theodore Beza. He allowed rebellion against a tyrant or an idolatrous ruler if it was led by the subordinate magistrates. He argued for a contract between people and ruler which allowed for the latter's deposition. He held that the subordinate magistrates could call for foreign aid. The non-resistance of apostolic days was necessary because then there was no proper way to challenge tyranny except private anarchy; if a Christian state had a system of subordinate magistrates the situation was quite different since their power, too, comes from God. As for religious belief, the magistrate may even risk peace to establish the pure service of God in his community.

Beza was not alone. In France, in Scotland, in England, in the Low Countries, Calvinist writers proclaimed similar, and more extreme opinions. The Crusade had come again. It is a long way from Erasmus to the *Soldiers' Catechism* of the English Civil War:

> Q. What Profession are you of?
> A. I am a Christian and a soldier.
> Q. Is it lawful for Christians to be soldiers?

A. Yea doubtless: we have arguments enough to warrant it...Almighty God declares himself a friend to our party...God now calls upon us to avenge the blood of his saints.[39]

Anarchism: the rejection of coercion

In recent years the political thinking of the English Civil War and Interregnum has attracted a very great deal of scholarly attention. Its common ground was Christianity but it would require a major study to discuss the many, varied, fluid and often self-contradictory attitudes to violence found at this time. Some of those involved, Oliver Cromwell among them, were deeply conscious of being, in Calvin's words, 'deliverers brought forward by the lawful call of God'. Others took the reformer's second proviso – the defence of liberty by its appointed guardians – and transformed it into theories of popular initiative which he would have disowned. But the hitherto little heard case for Anarchy does add a new dimension to the story of attitudes to violence, raising the fourth point of the compass of ideas, that force is evil and must be abandoned.

The most interesting exponent of this view was not the newly emerged Quaker movement, which did not avow pacifism until 1661, but the 'Digger', Gerrard Winstanley. Winstanley not only wrote, he acted, and in the spring of 1649 he appears as a leader of a small commune of 'Diggers' which set out to cultivate the waste land at Walton on Thames as the pilot project which would lead ultimately to the end of personal property. Their manifesto is quite explicit on violence:

Know this, that our blood and life shall not be unwilling to be delivered up in meekness to maintain universal liberty...and we shall not do this by force of arms, we abhor it, for that is the work of the Midianites, to kill one another; but by obeying the Lord of Hosts, who hath revealed himself in us and to us, by labouring the earth in righteousness together.[40]

The plan of the Diggers was to encourage the ordinary people to move on to the plentiful supply of uncultivated land and so leave existing society to collapse for lack of labour. The theoretical justification for this, in Winstanley, is that although society consisted of a minority with property and a majority without, this was the result of 'self-love' triumphing over 'universal love' because it held 'the power of the sword'. 'If every one did but quietly enjoy the earth for food and raiment, there would be no wars, prisons nor gallows.' Social and economic divisions are the result of force:

> The party that is called a king was but the head of an army, and
> he and his army having conquered, shuts the conquered out of
> the earth and will not suffer them to enjoy it, but as a servant
> and slave to him...the best you can say of kingly power that rules
> by the sword is this, he is a murderer and a thief.

By this date, of course, England was a republic and 'kingly power'
does not mean the rule of Charles I. It means the system of
property and privilege of which a king is the head and the
symbol.[41]

What was the remedy? Not violence:

> The way to cast out kingly power again is not to cast them out
> by the sword, for this doth but set him in more power and
> removes him from a weaker to a stronger hand. But the only
> way to cast him out is for the people to leave him to himself, to
> forsake fighting and all oppression and to live in love, one
> toward another. This power of love is the true saviour.

Man's only hope lay in rejecting covetousness and being prepared
to 'conquers all enemies by love and patience' by the strength of
his innate potential for good; 'I tell thee, thou England, thy battles
are all spiritual.' The whole principle of coercion –
'prisons, whips and gallows' – should disappear.[42]

Like Zwingli, however, Winstanley was not always consistent in
his approach to violence. He had supported parliament in its war
against the king, indeed he regarded the opening of the wastes and
commons to the people as the reward for their share in victory.
And the collapse of the Digger commune within a year, under
persecution and physical harassment, and a realization of the
realities of politics seem to have brought about a retreat in his
later writings from the principle of non-violence.

His blueprint for society, *The True Law of Freedom* (1652) accepts
the legitimate role of force in the community. Winstanley argues
that 'all state officers are soldiers, for they represent power; and if
there were not power in the hand of officers, the spirit of rudeness
would not be obedient to any law or government but their own
wills.' He also provides for the specialist role of policeman-*cum*-
warrior and for an army:

> A monarchical army lifts up mountains and makes valleys, viz.
> advances tyrants and treads the oppressed in the barren lanes of
> poverty. But a commonwealth's army is like John Baptist, who

levels the mountains to the valleys, pulls down the tyrant and lifts up the oppressed: and so makes way for the spirit of peace and freedom to come in to rule and inherit the earth.

In Winstanley's commonwealth there is 'whipping, imprisoning and death', and slavery. Was he, like Ferrovius in Shaw's play, *Androcles and the Lion*, an 'honest man who finds when the trumpet sounds that he cannot follow Jesus'?[43]

Yet despite this swing by Winstanley back towards an acceptance of the need for force in society, anarchist opposition to violence had been proclaimed, and it was still proclaimed. The Diggers' Song is unequivocal:

> To conquer them by love, come in now, come in now,
> To conquer them by love, come in now,
> To conquer them by love, as it does you behove,
> For he is king above, no power is like to love.
> Glory here, Diggers all.[44]

The sacrifice of righteousness

Holy war, Just War, renunciation of the world and the anarchy of love were all attempted in the hey-day and decline of Christian Europe. One of the certain conclusions which can be drawn from this discussion is the naivety of almost all Christian analyses of the problem of violence. Thinker after thinker approached the use of force from the starting-point of domestic order, but extended police action hardly characterizes most wars. Christian responses, too, are anything but simple and there is no single authoritative view. The crusading ideal is open to rapid debasement but it is the only position which attempts to express the truth that the world, though fallen, does belong to God and 'waits with eager expectation for God's sons to be revealed'.[45] The absolute pacifist is revealed as an exponent of contradiction, fundamentally incapable of coping with being in an ungodly world. But if we proclaim instead that violence is either part of the divine order or an expression of divine love we offer too much to the state. In other words, both pacifism and non-pacifism do violence to Christian morality.

It is not surprising that despite the dangers, so many thoughtful men have settled at last on the position of a pragmatic realism. It is pertinent to remember Dietrich Bonhoeffer's insight that for the Christian who is involved in the concerns of his own day, the supreme sacrifice he may have to make for Christ is his own righteousness.

Notes and references

1 Bernard Shaw, *Complete Plays*, Odhams, 1950, p. 703.

2 Latourette, *History of Christianity,* Eyre and Spottiswoode, 1954, p. 108.

3 J.R.Hale, 'War and Public Opinion in the Fifteenth and Sixteenth Centuries', in *Past and Present* 22, 1962, 19.

4 Fulcher of Chartres, quoted in R.Pernoud, Secker and Warburg, *The Crusades,* 1963, p. 26.

5 Latourette, *History of Christianity*, p. 456.

6 J.J.Hexter, *The vision of Politics on the Eve of the Reformation*, Basic Books, New York, 1973, p. 49.

7 J.Barnie, *War in Medieval Society 1337–99*, Weidenfield and Nicholson, 1974, p. 123.

8 L.U.Hanke, *Bartolomé de Las Casas* Martinus Nijhoff, The Hague, 1951, pp. 17, 45.

9 1 Corinthians 6 v. 12; J.B.Scott, *The Spanish Origin of International Law*, Clarendon Press, 1934, p. lxx.

10 Hanke, *op. cit.* p. 8.

11 Romans 13:3–4; J.M.Stayer, *Anabaptists and the Sword,* Coronado Press, Lawrence, Kansas, 1972, pp. 76–77.

12 *Ibid.* p. 84.

13 James Bisse, *Two Sermons Preached...the eight of January 1580,* 1585, sig. D7v.

14 *The Essential Erasmus*, ed. J.P.Dolan, Mentor–Omega, New York, 1964, pp. 191–2.

15 Scott, *op. cit.* pp. 44–45.

16 Hexter, *op. cit.* p. 54; *The Essential Erasmus*, p. 183.

17 R.W.Chambers, *Thomas More*, Jonathan Cape, 1938 edn., p. 121.

18 Scott, *op. cit.* p. 45.

19 Scott, *op. cit.* p. 47.

20 P. Brock, *The Political and Social Doctrines of the Unity of Czech Brethren,* Mouton and Co., The Hague, 1957, p. 47.

21 *Ibid.* pp. 55, 59.

22 *Ibid.* p. 219.

23 Stayer, *Anabaptists and the Sword*, p. 119.

24 P.J.Klassen, *The Economics of Anabaptism, 1525–60,* Mouton and Co., The Hague, 1964, pp. 126–27, 131.

25 J.W.Allen, *History of Political Thought in the Sixteenth Century*, Methuen, 1960, p. 46; E.Troeltsch, *The Social Teaching of the Christian Churches,* Allen and Unwin, 1931, 11.953.

26 *Luke* 22:38; Stayer, *Anabaptists and the Sword*, p. 37.

27 E.G.Rupp, *The Righteousness of God*, Hodder and Stoughton, 1953, pp. 296, 291–92; Stayer, *Anabaptists and the Sword*, p. 43.

28 Rupp, *Righteousness of God*, pp. 293, 297; Stayer, *Anabaptists and the Sword*, p. 43.

29 Rupp, *Righteousness of God*, p. 297; R.H.Bainton, *Studies in the Reformation,* Hodder and Stoughton, 1963, p. 41.

30 Stayer, *Anabaptists and the Sword*, p. 49.

31 *Ibid.* p. 58.

32 *Ibid.* p. 62; *New Cambridge Modern History*, ii, ed. G.R.Elton, Cambridge University Press, 1958, p. 102.

33 Stayer, *Anabaptists and the Sword*, p. 64.

34 *New Cambridge Modern History*, ii.103.

35 Allen, *History of Political Thought*, p. 53; John Calvin, *Institutes of the Christian Religion*, ed. H.Beveridge, Calvin Translation Society, Edinburgh, 1846, iii.530, 531, 533.

36 *Ibid.* iii.544.

37 *Ibid.* iii.551–52, 553.

38 Troeltsch, *Social teaching of the Christian Churches,* ii,920; Allen, *History of Political Thought*, p. 87.
39 Bainton, *Studies in the Reformation*, p. 273.
40 Gerrard Winstanley, *The Law of Freedom*, ed. Christopher Hill, Penguin Books, 1973, p. 83.
41 *Ibid.* pp. 192, 197.
42 *Ibid.* pp. 197, 271, 148, 201.
43 *Ibid.* pp. 333, 360, 335; Bernard Shaw, *Complete Plays*, p. 703.
44 Winstanley, *Law of Freedom*, p. 395.
45 Romans 8:22.

Chapter 13

The economic system: the capitalist connection

The student of history will not be long at his studies before he en-
counters the most famous of all the inter-relations between
Christianity and history, the linking of Protestantism with the rise
of capitalism. First attracting attention at the beginning of this
century, it has passed into popular orthodoxy. In academic circles,
too, it has become an unquestioned truth to many social scientists
and a basic assumption in many a text-book.

The theory is found in two forms. There is the initial hypothesis
advanced by Max Weber (1864–1920), notably in his essays 'The
Protestant Ethic and the Spirit of Capitalism' of 1904–5. For
Anglo-Saxon readers, Weber became well known only through the
famous *Religion and the Rise of Capitalism* (1926) in which the thesis
was expounded and developed by the doyen of British economic
historians, R.H.Tawney (1880–1962), but since then there has
been a massive and continuing academic debate. Secondly, and
arising from this academic presentation and discussion, there has
passed into general circulation the notion of a so-called 'protestant ethic', a formulation which even appears in analyses of our
contemporary highly secularized society.

Max Weber

Weber was interested in the comparative study of the social outlook and impact of different religions, 'the influence of certain
religious ideas on the development of an economic spirit, of the
ethos of an economic system'.[1] His analysis of Protestantism, the
most complete part of his work, has, therefore, a sharper outline
than if, as intended, it were part of a more comprehensive discussion of Western as against non-European cultures. It is also important to realize what Weber did *not* say, though he sometimes
gave his readers cause to think that he was saying: that Protestantism 'caused' capitalism, or that the economic factors leading to
capitalism could be ignored, or that capitalism had not existed
prior to the Reformation, indeed, that it had not 'existed in all

civilized countries of the earth', Eastern as well as Western, ancient and medieval as well as modern. Weber's thought is far more sophisticated.

In the history of the modern world capitalism has been of fundamental importance, but capitalism in a particular form, 'the rational bourgeois capitalism' which grew up in Western Europe from the sixteenth century. It can be distinguished from other forms of capitalism by its rationalism, the deliberate and calculated pursuit of profit as an end in itself, and by the consequent social change to a capitalist organization of formerly free labour. If this was so, what, Weber asked, was the pattern of ideas which allowed and encouraged this critical development? Where did this distinctive spirit of capitalism come from?

> It is only in the modern Western world that rational capitalistic enterprises with fixed capital, free labour, the rational specialization and combination of function, and the allocation of productive functions on the basis of capitalistic enterprises, bound together in a market economy are to be found.[2]

The mental climate for such a development Weber found in Protestantism, and particularly in what he called 'ascetic Protestantism', that is, Calvinism and notably the English puritan sects. Calvin made much of the idea that the Christian serves God in his daily vocation, in his 'calling'. However humble his employment, the Christian glorifies and serves God by doing it to the best of his ability, in a serious and responsible fashion. Coupled with this is a rejection of the luxuries and pleasures of the flesh and the result is, in Weber's term, 'worldly asceticism'. What Ernst Troeltsch (1865–1923) called 'the favourable ethical disposition of Calvinism for bourgeois capitalism' is obvious.[3] Troeltsch also points out that the traditional Christian exaltation of poverty is not thereby abandoned. Poverty witnesses to the spiritual danger which wealth threatens, and hence to the need to use wealth in Christian service, not in consumption.

What is the origin of this 'worldly asceticism', particularly since, with all Protestants, Calvin and the puritan sects scorned the notion that 'good works' can earn a man favour with God? An ethic of hard work is hardly a rational one. Weber's answer is to direct attention to two Protestant doctrines as crucial, the 'calling' and predestination. The doctrine of 'calling' has been mentioned already, with its consequence in the sober life of hard work and frugality. Predestination, the teaching that God has finally determined the eternal salvation or damnation of each individual before the person has even been born, works, according to Weber, in the same direction. Election to salvation could never be proved, but everything that happens in this world is at the will of God; therefore prosperity can easily be interpreted as the sign of God's favour, and the person seeking assurance of salvation readily slips into the habit of industry to ensure the prosperity which will authenticate his election.

R.H.Tawney

Although Tawney's views are frequently bracketed with those of Weber, giving us the 'Tawney-Weber hypothesis', he made a number of significant points of his own. He placed, for instance, more emphasis on the individualism of puritanism. He restated, in effect, Weber's conviction that economic movement and religious ideas operated in a reciprocal fashion, but in such a way as to avoid the need to look for a 'spirit of capitalism' in existence before 'capitalism'.

> It seems a little artificial to talk as though capitalist enterprise could not appear till religious changes had produced a capitalist spirit. It would be equally true, and equally one-sided, to say that the religious changes were purely the result of economic movements.[4]

With Weber, and against Marx, Tawney could hold that ideas and beliefs were not simply the product of the social system, but with Marx, and more emphatically perhaps than Weber, he could hold a belief in the formative effect of economic organization upon the whole of culture. Most important of all, Tawney introduced distinctions into Protestantism. He argued that in the first century of the Reformation, the elements in Protestantism favourable to capitalistic tendencies had been held back by the traditional conservatism common to all Christians. But in the later seventeenth century, tradition crumbled, and businessmen found their ideology in a Protestant ethic.

Realist alternatives

Given the quality of the minds which have taken part in the debate since Weber and Tawney first wrote, it may seem impudent to do anything other than immediately consider the discussion in detail. But before doing so, it is reasonable to be sure that there is a case to consider at all.

The only evidence for a connection between Protestantism and capitalism is circumstantial; the case rests on association. The most advanced economies in seventeenth and eighteenth century Europe were those of Britain and the Dutch Republic (the United Provinces), which were also the major Protestant powers outside the Lutheran tradition. Within communities of mixed religion, notably France, the Protestants were the more economically vigorous. But different associations can also be suggested.

Scotland and Switzerland were two regions where Calvinism also had success, but these did not develop bourgeois capitalism until late among European states. Perhaps the really significant feature shared by Britain and the Dutch Republic was not religion but being a beneficiary of a shift in the European economy which was confirmed and amplified by the opening up of the American and Asiatic trade. It is noticeable, too, that both countries were unusually free of government restrictionism and were tolerant in religion, and it is fair to point out that the most Calvinist area of the United Provinces was the least advanced economically.

Another possibility is that Protestantism often took root in an urban environment where, of course, bourgeois capitalism also has its roots. Is it that Protestantism and capitalism appear together because each belongs to the town? London was the centre for English capitalism in the seventeenth century; it was also the seed-bed of the Protestant sects. Another possibility is that social and political discrimination could have had the effect of driving religious minorities into the despised world of trade. This might apply to the non-conformists in England and the Huguenots in France. In turn, minorities could have become successful by reason of their cohesion (as with the English Quakers), or by the opportunity to keep out, or at least ahead of, would-be merchants of the majority religion (as seems to be true of the Huguenots). To adopt the terminology of the economist, these are all 'realist' explanations. They suggest, individually and collectively, plausible reasons for a coincidence of Protestantism and capitalism irrespective of religious belief.

One of the most challenging of 'realist' suggestions is that put forward by Hugh Trevor-Roper. He points out that many of the great financiers of seventeenth-century Europe are, at first sight, Dutch Calvinists. Their resources and their know-how were relied upon by all the powers of Europe, Catholic as well as Protestant. Gustavus Adolphus, Richelieu and, most incredible of all, the imperialist mercenary Wallenstein, each depended upon Calvinist expertise and Calvinist credit. But 'Calvinist' is an elastic term; by no means all these financiers were orthodox, and by no means all practised 'worldly asceticism'. Religion, in fact, is less significant than their places of origin. This was not, generally, Holland or other Calvinist territory, but Flanders. In other words, the Calvinist Dutch finance of the seventeenth century is the Flemish finance of the sixteenth, dispersed abroad and under a different name.

Those northern financiers who were not Calvinist also fit into the picture here, as again part of the Flemish diaspora. Related patterns can be traced elsewhere. In France, the financial origins go back, not to Antwerp, but to Southern Germany and the financiers of Augsburg; in Switzerland to the bankers of Northern Italy; in many places to the Jews from Lisbon and Seville. The capitalism of the seventeenth century has its roots in the medieval past.

> The techniques of capitalism applied in Protestant countries were not new. The century from 1520 to 1620 is singularly barren in new processes. The techniques brought by the Flemings to Holland, Sweden, Denmark, by the Italians to Switzerland and Lyons, were the old techniques of medieval capitalism, as perfected on the eve of the Reformation and applied to new areas.[5]

One problem which has always been recognized in Weber's thesis is the artificiality in drawing distinctions between the attitudes and careers of pre- and post-Reformation businessmen. If Trevor-Roper is correct, capitalism has been a continuum. The real problem then, is to explain why capitalists adhered to Protestantism or, when remaining Catholic, often chose to be based in Protestant territory. Part of the answer to this must be the well-established swing of Europe's economy towards a north which then changed to Protestantism. There is also an obvious importance in the policy of the Catholic powers towards the independent and anticlerical traditions of the commercial cities of Europe. As A.G.Dickens has said, they 'expelled their business classes or discouraged them to the point of emigration. From the economic viewpoint, Catholic Europe thus tended to emasculate itself and to transfer power to the Protestant North and, at least until Louis XIV began persecuting, to France'.[6]

Worldly asceticism

If realist arguments suggest other ways of explaining the occurrence together of Protestantism and capitalism, it is also possible to look more closely at capitalism itself, and to wonder whether it did benefit from an ethic of work and frugality. No doubt petty bourgeois could become rich by following such a way of life, but how much has thrift and low consumption to do with substantial capital accumulation or a large-scale capitalist system? The great opportunities for capitalism in the medieval period lay in servicing state and public finance, and the expansion of capitalism in the sixteenth and seventeenth centuries was a response to increasing opportunities in this same field. The state now needed credit on an ever increasing scale in order to survive in a world which demanded more and more of government but of government which had an insufficient financial and administrative base. B.E.Supple has written: 'The emergence of what appears to have been an *haute bourgeoisie* was a function of the existence of governments so constructed and motivated that their reach constantly exceeded their grasp'.[7]

It is, moreover, easy to exaggerate the bourgeois capitalism of sixteenth and seventeenth-century Europe. The demand made by the economy on the entrepreneur was not for investment so much as the financing of production on credit. The bulk of Western capital was still represented by the tools and simple machines of artisans who normally worked in their own houses. And where major investment was required, notably in metals and mining, capital organization was simple and often short-term. The usual pattern, Europe-wide, was not the speculative entrepreneur acting alone, but the landowner, his neighbours, the merchant and others with money to invest (such as the lawyer) acting in partnership. Opportunities for capitalistic enterprise were undoubtedly becoming more common, but through the sixteenth and much of the seventeenth century, a great deal of Europe's capitalism seems to belong to the world of the shopkeeper or the co-operation of friends.

Legitimating usury

It is often alleged that sixteenth-century Calvinism encouraged capitalism by allowing the payment of interest upon loans. The medieval church, so the argument goes, prohibited usury; 'money does not beget money.' Luther was a conservative on the subject and repeated tradition. Calvin, on the other hand, recognized that usury was not necessarily evil, and so opened the floodgates to capitalism.

Closer scrutiny of theory and practice gives a more complicated picture. Medieval commerce certainly tolerated the charging of interest on loans, although often in a disguised form. Theory, with the peasant and the money-lender in mind, maintained a strict prohibition on usury, on the natural-law argument that usury is theft; the lender insists on being paid back more than he originally lent. But a lender's right to compensation, 'interest', was recognized in certain circumstances, especially for loss – such as delay in repayment – or for being deprived of the use of his money. Thus the real thrust of much scholastic thinking was against taking exorbitant interest under these exceptions. It is noteworthy that the church, especially the Franciscan friars, promoted *monti di pieta*, in effect 'small-loan' banks, which lent to the poor at minimum rates; these received papal approval in 1516. The *rente*, nominally a form of rent charge or mortgage, was given limited sanction by Pope Martin V as early as 1425 and by the middle of the next century the device was well established in Spain and France (still, of course, Catholic countries). In 1543 the Emperor Charles V, that pillar of orthodoxy, extended official approval of interest to the Netherlands.

Luther's views, as so often, are coloured by his awareness of the contrast between the Christian ideal and worldly realities. On the one hand, therefore, his condemnation of usury was more rigorous than that of the late-medieval canon lawyers. He argued that the *rente* was unjust because all the risk was on the borrower – the creditor always got his money; it was also contrary to Christ's instruction to lend without expecting to be repaid. On the other hand, Luther did admit that charging interest was, in practice, justified in certain circumstances, especially where large sums were involved. Yet his concern is with the small borrower and he shows little interest in the nature of the commercial loan.

> The smaller the percentage the more godly and Christian the contract...It is my opinion, however, that if we tried to keep Christ's commandment...the *rente* contract would not be so common or so necessary, except in cases where the amounts were very considerable and the properties large.
> But it has made its way into the groats and pennies, and deals with insignificant sums that could easily be dispensed by gifts or [free] loans in accordance with Christ's commandment. Yet it refuses to be called greed!

Exorbitant rates drew his wrath:

> There are some who charge too high a rate: 7, 8, 9, or 10 per cent. The rulers ought to look into this. Here the poor common folk are secretly fleeced and severely oppressed. This is also why these robbers and usurers often die an unnatural and sudden death.

Luther's *Table Talk* records the comment, 'I am happy to concede what the law and the Emperor allow – namely 5 or 6 per cent. But 20, 30 and 40 per cent – this is excessive'.[8]

Against this background, Calvin seems less an innovator and more a clarifier of the problem. What he does is to distinguish money-lending from investment, the loan for consumption from the business loan, and to argue that the scriptural prohibitions against usury simply do not refer to the latter.

> Whoever asks a loan of me does not intend to keep the money idle and gain nothing. The profit is not in the money itself [against the argument that 'money does not beget money'] but in the return that comes from its use.

> If any rich and monied man, wishing to buy a piece of land, should borrow some part of the sum required of another, may not he who lends the money receive some part of the revenues of the farm until the principal shall be repaid?[9]

For the non-commercial loan all the old prohibitions remain in force. Only where a profit is made is interest justified.

This is really little more than a reformulation of the medieval permission for some payment to be made to the creditor for not being able to use his money for the period of the loan. Calvin is saying that the creditor is entitled to part of the gains his money makes possible. Calvin's practice, too, is much like that of the medieval church. He is concerned to keep interest rates low and to protect the poor. He wrote: 'since men cannot otherwise transact their business, we must always observe what is lawful and how far it is so'.[10] Calvin was familiar with the facts of Genevan economic life and all his influence seem to have been directed to prevent the abuse of interest, not to prohibit it, still less to encourage the system. There appears to be little difference in practice between countries under his, and those under Lutheran or Catholic influence.

There is no ground, therefore, for asserting that Calvin's writings mark a turning-point in European attitudes towards usury, or for the belief that usury and Protestantism go hand in hand. There is also doubt whether the general toleration of usury, for whatever reason, had much significance for the development of capitalism. Certainly capitalism is inconceivable without interest being paid in some form, but it is obvious that the excessive rates which were the main target of the criticisms of the schoolmen, Luther and Calvin alike, were no inducement to

capitalistic enterprise. To the extent that lower interest rates encourage investment, all efforts to promote them had implications
for economic growth, whether or not agitators were aware of this.
But since the critics were arguing against the background of very
high rates, their limited toleration of usury could have been little
encouragement to capitalist enterprise. What changed the situation
was a new mobilization of credit, with the result that, for example,
maximum rates of interest in England fell from an initial 10 per cent
in 1545 and 1571 to 6 per cent after 1651.

One possibility, of course, would be that the change in attitudes
implied by this increase in credit available was a delayed result of
Calvin's justification of usury in commerce. But interest rates in
orthodox Spain fell from a maximum on *censos* (i.e. *rentes*) of 15
per cent in the early sixteenth century to 5 per cent after 1608; in
Genoa, 5 per cent in the 1520s had become 1$\frac{1}{2}$ per cent after 1604.
What is more, Calvin's very limited approval of the interest-
bearing business loan did not win wide support among his fellow
Protestants. The note struck by preacher and pamphleteer alike
was far more usually that of the traditional condemnation of
usury. This was understandable enough in England where most
men knew the traditional evil of the money-lender, and not the
business man wishing to invest, but less so in the Netherlands. Yet
the puritans of Bury in Lancashire declared in 1647 that 'usury is a
scandalous sin', and in Holland, the financial centre of the world,
bankers were not admitted to holy communion until 1658.[11] Since,
therefore, changes in attitude towards investment took place
across Europe, irrespective of a country's religious posture, and
since in Calvinist circles any move towards relaxation was in
defiance of the teaching of the church, it is hard to see that
Calvin's lucid identification of the loan for production had much
effect.

The psychology of Protestantism

Faced with realist explanations for the growth of modern capitalism, explanations which can be tested empirically in the way
historians prefer, it may seem strange that scholars have been so
fascinated with the possible role of Protestantism. Weber was concerned to vindicate the non-materialistic influences on history, but
it is not unjust to suspect that, for others, the attraction has been
the chance to reduce religious conviction to an element in
sociology.

Interest has concentrated upon the two psychological
mechanisms which Weber saw in Calvinism, the way men

responded to the doctrines of predestination and calling. The first can be dismissed without more ado as highly improbable. It is true that some men were tortured by doubts about their own election, but their response was despair, not good works to convince themselves that they did belong to the elect. The cruellest element in strict Calvinism was that it told the despairing that it was perfectly possible that his despair was warranted. Predestination is a psychological spur for those who know they are saved, not for those who fear they are damned. The puritan dynamic comes from a conscious commitment in response to the divine election, a doing of God's will because that is what being a Christian is all about. The puritan morale which swept away monarchy in England did not begin in a desire to quieten fears about eternity, but in acceptance of the obligation on the elect to follow 'the Lord's leading'. Even though, as Christopher Hill has argued, this could often mean following the logic of events, it was not a passive Micawberism but a readiness to force the pace.

There is far more substance in Weber's second suggestion, that the doctrine of calling can determine economic attitudes. Clearly, if the whole of a person's life is regarded as service to God, attitudes of responsibility, sobriety, diligence and honesty necessarily follow. As defined by William Perkins (1558–1602), a vocation or calling 'is a certain kind of life, ordained and imposed on man by God, for the common good'.[12]

But two points can be made about the importance of the calling. First, although it was more emphasized after than before the Reformation, and by Protestants rather than Catholics, the idea belongs really to the common stock of Christianity. It is not exclusive to Calvinism, still less to Protestantism; after all, the deadly sin of sloth was a favourite theme of medieval preachers and moralists.

Secondly, the concept of calling is a restriction on human activity, not a call to self-expression. As Tawney strongly emphasized, puritanism sought, until the Civil War, to increase discipline in the community; 'it would have been scandalized by economic individualism'. In particular, the pursuit of wealth for its own sake was roundly condemned; a 'sufficiency', estimated according to 'the common judgement and practice of the most godly, frugal and wise men with whom we live' was all that William Perkins would allow. Furthermore,

> our riches must be employed to necessary uses. These are first, the maintenance of our own good estate and condition.

Secondly, the good of others, specially those that are of our family or kindred...Thirdly, the relief of the poor...Fourthly, the maintenance of the Church of God...Fifth, the maintenance of the Commonwealth.[15]

A doctrine of calling certainly sanctified worthy human activity, but it did so by subjecting that activity to a rigorous Christian scrutiny. Any increase in the attention which puritan preachers gave to the subject simply indicates how determined they were to retain the increasingly restive world of business under the domination of the Christian ethic.[13]

Neo-Calvinism and the justification of profit

It was R.H.Tawney's recognition that puritan teaching was initially restrictive which caused him to make a very important modification of Weber's original hypothesis, perhaps following a hint from Ernst Troeltsch. Troeltsch had suggested that there was a difference between primitive Calvinism and later, or neo-Calvinism, what Calvinism became under the influence of 'sect-type' Christianity and the need to adjust to being a denomination, not a state church. Tawney now argued for a substantial shift in puritan attitudes on economic matters in the later years of the seventeenth century which allowed the encouragements to capitalism, always inherent in Calvinism, to escape the previous restraints.

Discarding the suspicion of economic motives, which had been as characteristic of the reformers as of medieval theologians, Puritanism in its later phases added a halo of ethical sanctification to the appeal of economic expediency, and offered a moral creed, in which the duties of religion and the calls of business ended their long estrangement in an unanticipated reconciliation.[14]

That there was some shift in puritan attitudes in the later seventeenth century may be admitted; the question is, in what direction, how far and under what impulse? The direction, it seems clear, was not towards the stock exchange but the shop. *The Tradesman's Calling* (1684) by the nonconformist preacher Richard Steele (1629–92) certainly encourages the business ethic:

Next to the saving his soul, [the tradesman's] care and business is to serve God in his calling, and to drive it as far as it will go.

But as the title suggests, the author is not writing for the would-be entrepreneur. Tawney was well aware of this, and argued that this reflected the fact that 'the centre of economic gravity' had not yet shifted from the small artisan or trader to 'the exporting merchant, the industrial capitalist and the financier'. Nevertheless, the vital connection between profit and Christianity had been made.

> Between the old-fashioned denunciation of uncharitable covetousness and the new-fashioned applause of economic enterprise, a bridge is thrown by the argument which urges that enterprise itself is the discharge of a duty imposed by God.[15]

This is really to exaggerate the extent to which enterprise had become acceptable. Steele preserves powerful restrictions:

> Direct all to a right, the honour of God, the Public Good as well as your Private Commodity, and then every step and stroke in your Trade is sanctified. You are working for God, who will be sure to reward you to your heart's content.

Richard Baxter (1615–91) who also accommodated certain parts of the strict puritan tradition to the realities of business, nevertheless warned that riches were an obstacle to salvation 'and the love of this world is the commonest cause of men's damnation'. John Wesley, in his sermon 'The Use of Money', published in 1746, advised his hearers to acquire wealth and to save it, but hedged this advice with a whole pallisade of moral criteria, and finally he announced the purpose of such diligence:

> Having, first, gained all you can, and secondly, saved all you can, then 'give all you can'...Employ whatever God has entrusted you with, in doing good, all possible good, in every possible kind and degree, to the household of faith, to all men![16]

Neo-Calvinism: cause or effect?

What about the impetus for this very cautious shift towards the interests of the small trader? Why did Christian ministers write and preach like this? Hardly one imagines to promote commerce and commercial values. It is far more likely that they were responding to the needs of puritan tradesmen caught up in an increasing velocity of business life. It is an example of the eternal dilemma of the church, whether to cling to a purism made impossible by new situations, or whether to compromise in the hope of retaining some influence. Or, to be fairer to the Christians involved, how to make the gospel meet the needs of seeking people for whom traditional absolutes are not a real option. In the brewery town, the total-abstainer who preaches prohibition will be irrelevant to a congregation which directly and indirectly is dependent on the industry he attacks.

Even if Tawney was right to suggest that the later puritans, the neo-Calvinists, to adopt Troeltsch's convenient label, did legitimate the profit motive in England – and examples of the proverb 'give an inch and lose a yard' are not unknown in history – a basic difficulty still remains. Towards the end of the seventeenth century, Europe was passing through the intellectual turmoil we somewhat inadequately describe as 'the Scientific Revolution', but which Hazard more aptly entitled, 'the crisis of European consciousness'.[17] How is the historian to be sure that it is neo-Calvinism which is the effective agent in promoting capitalist ethics and not the universal wind of change? Indeed, perhaps neo-Calvinism itself is a product of that pressure. If Weber is correct in identifying rationalism as the critical element in bourgeois capitalism, then ascetic Protestantism is not the only or the most plausible candidate for parent. It seems very probable that whatever changes occurred in Protestant thinking about economic morality were a response to changing attitudes towards business and to a general secularization of life.

A mental revolution

In recent years, the most interesting discussion of the Protestant-capitalist connection in England's past has come from the pen of Christopher Hill. He accepts that there is a 'Protestant ethic', but he moves the centre of attention back to the puritanism of the later sixteenth and earlier seventeenth century. There, puritanism was one of the factors which combined to challenge the old, monarchical, feudal society and its attitudes, ultimately on the field of battle. As we have seen, Hill believes that the psychology of predestination is direct and positive, not an inversion of doubt, but he still considers the puritan stress upon calling as vital. The moral imperative was to serve God and others through responsible labour, and hence 'productive economic activity' was good in itself. Idleness was plainly a sin and the rituals and restrictions of tradition were to be judged and rejected at the bar of individual conscience.

However, the importance of puritanism to Christopher Hill is more in its overall challenge to established ideas than in any one particular doctrine.

> The hold over men's minds of an established doctrinal system had to be broken before the political and social order sanctified by those doctrines could be challenged...there is nothing in Protestantism which leads automatically to capitalism: its importance was rather that it undermined obstacles which the more rigid institutions and ceremonies of Catholicism imposed...The Protestant revolt melted down the iron ideological framework which held society in its ancient mould.

The critical element in Protestantism was 'that in any given society it enabled religion to be moulded by those who dominated in that society'. This is not so much to develop the ideas of Weber and Tawney as to assimilate them to the position on religion argued by Marx.

> There was no inherent theological reason for the Protestant emphasis on frugality, hard work, accumulation; but that emphasis was a natural consequence of the religion of the heart in a society where capitalist industry was developing.

Protestant ideology is the medium through which the new values could permeate society.[18]

A particular strength of Hill's case is that he faces up to a problem too often overlooked in this whole debate, the problem of the extent of puritan influence. It is hard to believe that many, let alone a majority, of Englishmen sat under a regular puritan ministry, although the opportunities for this were clearly much greater for Londoners and other townsmen. And amongst those who listened, only a proportion would have committed themselves to the puritan way, strewn as it was by the preachers with the rocks of scrupulousness.

Hill contends, however, that many of the religious positions which committed puritans occupied seemed to make good worldly sense to the bourgeoisie. Sabbath observance and the negative of this, the ending of saints' days as holidays, would suit anyone interested in a rhythm of steady production. The puritan emphasis on the authority and obligations of the head of the household would appeal to an employer in an age when 'family' was taken to include servants as well as relations. Puritanism, that is, became a focus for the 'industrious, middling sort of people' although as individuals they might not be involved with puritan theology and, indeed, might reject much of it.

As an explanation of the nature of the support enjoyed by puritanism in the England of Elizabeth and the early Stuarts, this formulation is distinctly helpful. It is not, of course, restricted to social and economic matters; puritanism, for instance, was the ideology of nationalism. But where does this leave 'the Protestant ethic'?

Business ethic or Protestant ethic?

Until the Restoration and after, the primary emphasis of preachers was on the social morality of an individual's work, and this, as we have seen, was a restriction, not a liberation. It may be human nature to listen if we like what we hear and to shut our ears if we do not, but this is no comment on the speaker. As Hill himself has said of 'capitalist man': 'At worst the preachers clothed his nakedness in a fig-leaf of hypocrisy; at best they humanized some industrial relations and directed energy towards public service as well as private profit'.[19] Protestantism, in other words was the victim, not the villain. It was plundered by the business community to suit its interests. We should talk of a 'business ethic', not a 'Protestant ethic'. The ethic was Protestant only to the extent that the commercial classes chose a religious expression of their philosophy.

This gives no ground for the beating of breasts at the blindness of men to the gospel. The system of appointing puritans as salaried lecturers in urban centres meant that the desire of a preacher to minister in a way relevant to his congregation was often reinforced by a dependence on that congregation for his income. Puritans were also clearly willing to ally with the forces of change to reach particular objectives, without discussing principles. Puritans, that is, entered into unholy alliances. But they were alliances and nothing more. The considerable variety in the ethic of ascetic Protestantism in different parts of Europe must be remembered here. This variety is a reflection of contrasting circumstances: what happened to English puritanism as against continental 'puritanism' is an indication not of an inherent malleability in Protestantism but of the difference in context.

Christopher Hill is undoubtedly correct in bringing puritanism back into the story of the English Revolution. We may agree that puritans helped to undermine the existing authority, only to discover to their horror that they had undermined the principle of authority. No doubt they offered a religious programme which made sense and won them support on secular grounds. Perhaps a wilful selection and distortion of puritan teaching could have helped an acquisitive individual to some kind of self-justification. But capitalism and Protestantism are linked only by associations of this sort, not by cause and effect, however interpreted.

The development of Protestantism and the growth and elaboration of business, these are two vigorous climbers in the soil of early-modern Europe. Intertwined, sometimes hanging the one on the other, they are distinct, from separate roots and essentially in competition. Indeed, to extend the metaphor, it was only when the true genus *protestant ethic* withered, that the genus *business ethic* began to grow unchecked, and ironically to take the name of the species it had helped to choke.

The blight of orthodoxy

Without interpretation, history is worthless. Even a hypothesis which is ultimately abandoned retains an enduring significance in the research it stimulated, the research that ultimately destroyed it. But a hypothesis which becomes an orthodoxy, an axiom, is a blight on the subject. And this, it may be suggested, has been the fate of the Weber-Tawney hypothesis connecting the Protestant ethic and the spirit of the entrepreneur, religion and the rise of capitalism. There has been enormous value in the discussion of the relationship, but the link is not established, quite the reverse.

It is time to stop trying to fit analysis into the Weber-Tawney framework and more than time to drop the easy reference to the 'Protestant ethic' as an accepted fact, when at best it is unproven, unprovable and highly improbable.

Notes and references

1 M.Weber, *The Protestant Ethic and the Spirit of Capitalism*, Allen and Unwin, 1930, p. 27.

2 M.J.Kitch, *Capitalism and the Reformation*, Allen and Unwin, 1967, p. xvii.

3 E.Troeltsch, *The Social Teaching of the Christian Churches*, 1931, ii.812.

4 R.H.Tawney, *Religion and the Rise of Capitalism*, J. Murray, 1936, p. 320.

5 H.R.Trevor-Roper, 'Religion, the Reformation and Social Change', extracts in Kitch, *Capitalism and the Reformation*, p. 36.

6 A.G.Dickens, *Reformation and Society in Sixteenth-Century Europe,* Thames and Hudson, 1966, p. 180.

7 B.E.Supple, 'The Great Capitalist Man-hunt', in *Business History* vi, 1963, 56.

8 Martin Luther, *Works*, ed. J.Pelikan *etc.* Fortress Press, Philadelphia, 1958–67, 45.305; 54.369.

9 John Calvin, 'Letter to Claude de Sachins,' 1545, cited in H.M.Robertson, *Aspects of the Rise of Economic Individualism*, Cambridge University Press, 1933, p. 116; *Commentaries on the Four Last Books of Moses*, ed. C.W.Bingham, Calvin Translation Society, 1852, i.151.

10 John Calvin, *Commentary on Ezekiel*, ed. T. Myers, Calvin Translation Society, 1850, ii.228.

11 Tawney, *Religion and the Rise of Capitalism*, p. 218.

12 William Perkins, *Works*, 1626, i.750.

13 Tawney, *Religion and the Rise of Capitalism*, p. 213; Perkins, *Works*, ii.12.

14 Tawney, *Religion and the Rise of Capitalism*, pp. 239–40.

15 *Ibid.* p. 246, 244, 247.

16 *Ibid.* p. 92; Kitch, *Capitalism and the Reformation*, p. 114; John Wesley, *Forty-four Sermons*, Epworth Press, 1944, pp. 586, 588.

17 P.Hazard, *La Crise de la Conscience Européenne* (Paris, 1935), translated as *The European Mind, 1680–1715*, Hollis and Carter, 1953.

18 Christopher Hill, 'Protestantism and the Rise of Capitalism', in *Essays in the Economic and Social History of Tudor and Stuart England*, ed. F.J.Fisher, Cambridge University Press, 1961, pp. 35–36.

19 *Ibid.* p. 39.

Chapter 14

The dignity of man: the laity and the church, 1500–1660

The church is out of step with many of the cultural trends of the later twentieth century. Where society is becoming more egalitarian, the church clings to a hierarchy; where society is becoming more democratic, the church retains much of its authoritarianism; where society is concerned about the status of women, the church regards them as inferior; where differences in wealth, culture and colour of skin matter more than ever, the church has not shed its white, Westernizing image. True, this is a severe catalogue – the position is improving; true, there are exceptions. But as long as the over-all appearance is of an organization run by white, Western, male priests, ruled by appointed, monarchical bishops or other leaders, so long the impression will remain. And it is strengthened by much social analysis which portrays the church as a keystone of the establishment, a mechanism for ideological conditioning in support of the status quo. Again the charge is overstated, but the element of truth has made it an axiom of the political left.

Criticism of this kind is not new, as witness the enduring phenomenon of anticlericalism. This is not necessarily anti-religious. Although in the French and Russian Revolutions it did take on this complexion, in the English Revolution the contrast was between the established church in collaboration with a restrictive state and social order, and the true freedom of Christ. In parts of the Third World today, Christianity can be seen both as an oppressive force and as a faith for revolutionaries.

But whatever the form, anticlericalism is evidence of the rejection of an ecclesiastical system which seems an authoritarian institution of privilege, an organisation which treats the laity as second class. Cardinal Gasquet used to tell of an enquirer who asked (in the days before the Second Vatican Council) about the position of the laity in the Roman Catholic church. 'The layman', a priest told him, 'has two positions. He kneels before the altar, that is one. And he sits below the pulpit, that is the other'. 'And', said

Gasquet, 'there is one more. The layman also puts his hand into his purse.'

Clergyman and layman: the widening gap

There was, of course, an inevitability about the development of a special status for the clergy. The priest was a man apart. Ideally he had to be able to read; probably he was the only literate person in the community. The priest had a special place in the divine scheme of things, he had special supernatural authority. Yet it is also undeniable that the self-interest of the organized clergy drove towards the same goal. The text from Deuteronomy, 'Thou shalt not plough with an ox and an ass together', had been applied to the division of clergy and laity as early as AD 619, and the reorganization of the church initially associated with Hildebrand, Pope Gregory VII (1073–85), accentuated this contrast.[1] The ruler, who in the early medieval period had played an important part in the church, was now excluded and a specific attempt was made to divorce the church from lay interference, for instance by setting up separate courts for the clergy.

The greater definition of the sacraments which also took place, for example the definition of transubstantiation by the Lateran Council of 1215, helped to elevate the position of those who administered them. Traditional customs, such as lay confession, became more and more rare and, again in 1215, all laymen were ordered to confess once a year to a priest. Increasing educational standards, especially of the higher clergy, worked in the same direction. The result was a church effectively identified with the body of the clergy. As Stephen Langton, Archbishop of Canterbury, said in 1213, 'Because you are layfolk, it is your business to believe that your prelates are men who do all things discreetly and with counsel'.[2]

The laity were second class citizens of the Kingdom of God. They could find significance only in serving the church. The role of the feudal warrior, for example, was to protect the church and, in the Crusades, to protect Christendom from the infidels. The ideal Christian was the monk; the highest expression of Christian living was withdrawal from the world.

Lay protest: medieval initiatives

But it would be wrong to see caste and privilege as a necessary feature of the Christian community; it was challenged even in the High Middle Ages when the church was at the peak of its authority. The laity never wholly accepted their inferior role, and an element in medieval heresy was precisely the protest of laymen against the denial of their part in the church. It is not always easy to be certain about medieval heresy; we are largely dependent on the evidence of enemies. Another complication is that as church authorities became conscious of heresy, they tended to see it everywhere. Erasmus complained of the habit of labelling people heretics on flimsy grounds, and London became very angry in 1514 when it thought that a merchant, Richard Hunne, had been charged with heresy in retaliation for his attacks on the privileges of the clergy. Nevertheless the element of lay protest in heresy is there.

Particularly interesting for understanding attitudes towards the clergy is the flagellant movement of the thirteenth to the fifteenth century. Under church control in southern Europe, elsewhere it was always suspect. It reached a peak in Germany in the year of the Black Death, 1348–49. Very large numbers were involved, and fresh bands of penitents, fifty to five hundred strong, were arriving at Strassburg for six months on end. Each had a distinctive uniform, but the organization was standard. The leader of each group was called 'Master' or 'Father', and had to be a layman; he heard confessions, imposed penances and granted absolution. The ceremony of flagellation (corporate, public scourging) took place outside a church, with the flagellants forming a circle, and if a priest entered the circle, the rite was null and void. Those taking part sang hymns in the vernacular, the first non-Latin liturgical forms in the West since the collapse of the Roman Empire. As the movement became more uncontrolled it became more actively anticlerical, especially in Germany, but it is this offer of substitute lay ceremonies which is so significant. Faced with anarchy, the pope ceased to countenance the flagellants. He condemned them in a bull of 1349 and thus encouraged, the secular authorities stamped out the movement by force.

Lay protest was also a feature of certain non-fanatical and clearly Christian movements which were nevertheless proscribed as heretical. Peter of Bruys (near Aix en Provence) held that the living Spirit of God was more important than the forms, ceremonies and disciplines of the church and he attacked the ecclesiastical hierarchy; he was burned in 1137 but his followers, the Petrobrusians, lingered on. More numerous were the Waldensians who survived to become one of the Protestant communions at the Reformation. Started in about 1177 by a Lyons merchant, Peter Waldo, they were forbidden by the church to preach, disobeyed the order and were excommunicated in 1184. Among their tenets were belief that women and laymen had the right to preach, and that laymen were competent to hear confession and, if necessary, to administer the eucharist. They also rejected the liturgy and argued that the authority of a cleric depended upon his morality, not his orders. Closely associated with these 'Poor Men of Lyons' were the 'Humiliati' who centred on the cloth workers of Northern Italy. The pattern with these groups is very clear. Beginning as lay movements for voluntary poverty and Bible reading they incur ecclesiastical hostility and then throw out more extreme manifestations of anticlericalism. In many ways it was the clumsiness of church authority which brought about the progression to heresy.

One popular movement which avoided this fate was, of course, that started by Francis of Assisi. A son of a wealthy merchant, he felt called to embrace poverty and to reach the masses with the gospel, living a life of literal imitation and obedience of and to Christ. The group which gathered round him, the Penitents of Assisi, were laymen and Francis himself was never more than a deacon. When Francis and his followers became a recognized order in the church, lay brothers were a vital part of the structure while a 'Third Order' consisted of lay people in ordinary life who took vows to practise asceticism and do works of charity and penitence. But this pioneering effort to provide for the laity inside the religious community and outside in the world did not last for long after Francis died in 1226. By about 1242 the recruitment of laymen was forbidden.

The Reformation lay protest

Whether proscribed, or not by the church, such medieval phenomena were, in part, lay protests against a church which treated the layman as an inferior creature. The Reformation itself was a continuation of that protest, although there was obviously more to the movement than merely lay unrest. A number of points illustrate this.

Anticlericalism was, without doubt, the most potent force in the Reformation. In the Middle Ages there was always some jealousy and fear of a class which had an esoteric monopoly, but the elevation of the pretensions of the clergy in later medieval Europe and the growing wealth of the church, coupled with its lack of spiritual vigour and its concentration on legalism, all tended to produce a particularly bitter brand of criticism. The German Peasants' War of 1524–25 was substantially directed against ecclesiastical landlords. In England the classic example is the case of the merchant Richard Hunne, and Simon Fish and William Tyndale were only the most vehement of literary anticlericals. Tyndale cried: 'the parson sheareth, the vicar shareth, the parish priest polleth, the friar scrapeth and the pardoner pareth; we lack but a butcher to pull off the skin'.[3]

Anticlericalism was becoming more intense because of a growing feeling that the clergy were a parasitic class. Monasticism, in particular, seemed irrelevant and out of date. The arrival of the literate layman in Western Europe had destroyed the practical distinction between layman and cleric which had helped to protect the claim of the clergy to be theologically distinct. In the fifteenth century the clerical monopoly of writing and reading first declined and was then extinguished by the arrival of the printing press.

Renaissance values
The feeling that the old status of the clergy was an anachronism was also fed by the spread of new moral values, the Renaissance. This was essentially the discovery of a justification for the active secular life. Contact with classical literature revealed a world where the ascetic life of the church was not the ideal. Instead it was the good life lived in normal society which was morally justified and worthwhile – self development for social improvement and the pursuit of wealth for the quality of living it made possible. The whole notion was embodied in a new educational philosophy. Education was no longer to be vocational training for the priesthood. The goal now was the development of the personality, character and ability of the individual, under the influence of the moral philosophy of antiquity, to make men good and useful in their station in life. The whole basis of Renaissance ideas was deeply Christian, but it was not clerical Christianity but lay Christianity which benefitted.

Lay self-help
The Reformation is not only a lay protest against the standards of the clergy and a rebellion against the excessive distinction between clergy and laity, it shares with the earlier 'heretical' phenomena the character of lay self-help. There is, for example, a clear historical connection between the reform of the sixteenth century and the heretical movements of John Wycliffe and Jan Hus at the end of the fourteenth and beginning of the fifteenth. There is an even clearer connection, clearer because not confused by the heresy issue, between the Reformation and the Brethren of the Common Life and similar late medieval free religious associations and

groups, predominantly lay in character and practising a Christianity of and for the man in the street.

In England, before the break with Rome there was a significant amount of religious heterodoxy, concentrated on Bible reading and personal piety. This strain continued through the reigns of Henry VIII and his children and into the seventeenth century. When the crown seemed to be offering a satisfactory religious pattern, the strain weakened, but whenever Christians became frustrated by established religion, they would again set out to provide their own. On the Essex-Suffolk border, for example, there was a hotbed of Lollard heresy in the later Middle Ages, the burning of martyrs even under Henry VIII, a protestant group that wished to go faster than the government of Edward VI, an underground church and more martyrs under Mary, a centre of advanced puritanism under Elizabeth and a major export of nonconformists to America in the next century.

A more striking example of lay initiative comes from Salzburg. Lutheran reform was preached there in 1519 but persecution in 1527 drove the converts underground. They organized worship in private houses since they had no churches, and they were also without ministers or any regular provision of the sacraments. It was not, however, until 1732 that the group was finally expelled, having survived for two centuries without a clergy.

Lay leadership

Laymen were, therefore, engaged in the Reformation as critics and as religious 'do-it-yourself' enthusiasts. They were also a dominant factor in shaping the Reformation. This is clearly true of the prince or 'godly magistrate' who managed to recover all, and perhaps more than all the ancient imperial status in the church. But the ruler is a special case. More significant was the emergence of the laity in church government. This was most noticeable in Calvinism, with its association of lay elders in church discipline, but it is found elsewhere.

In England religious conformity was the responsibility of the lay magistrate and his was the major initiative, and this was true even of the Marian persecution. From the middle of the sixteenth century, England had a parliamentary religion, whether Catholic or Protestant, and the note of lay assertion is heard in the famous encounter between Peter Wentworth and Archbishop Parker over the enacting of the Thirty Nine Articles in 1571. Wentworth reported his reply when Parker asked why the Commons had excluded certain items:

'Surely, Sir,' said I, 'because we were so occupied in other matters that we had no time to examine them, how they agreed with the word of God.'

'What!' said he, 'surely you mistook the matter. You will refer yourselves wholly to us therein.'

'No, by the faith I bear unto God!' said I, 'we will pass nothing before we understand what it is, for that were but to make you Popes. Make you Popes who list,' said I, 'for we will make you none.'[4]

Luther affirmed the right of the congregation to depose an unsuitable preacher, but in the Calvinist tradition the notion of 'calling' the minister to a church gave the laity some voice in selecting him. In the Anglican church, where so many of the impropriations (the right to present a clergyman to a living) were in lay hands and could be bought and sold, the lay patron and sometimes even the whole parish would choose the parson. In the radical congregations this went even further, with full and equal rights for laity, women no less than men.

The Catholic church also, though less affected, was not entirely exempt. The laity played a prominent part under Pope Paul III (1534–49) in the first period of the Council of Trent, and some were promoted directly to the rank of cardinal. Ignatius Loyola began the Society of Jesus as a layman and with laymen. In Elizabethan England and after, the particular circumstances made Catholic clergy completely dependent upon the shelter offered by the laity, and it is clear that this ultimately changed a heroic mission to convert the English into a service given to an isolated group of recusant gentry.

Meeting the need

The Reformation also saw much attention given to the spiritual needs of the laity, whether amongst the Catholics or the Protestants. Services were once more designed with them in mind. The Council of Trent insisted on a much clearer performance of the liturgy. Luther produced his German mass, Cranmer his prayer book. Hymns became more common, there was an emphasis on catechisms and a new stress on preaching. In Protestant circles the Bible was of dominant importance, with the attempt to make the vernacular scriptures available to all. Puritans, in particular, developed the practice of private and family prayer. In the Catholic church experience seemed to teach the danger of lay initiative, so all lay religious societies were suppressed and household religion discouraged. Instead, the laity were organized and drilled into a regular performance of routine parochial religion. But if the result was different, the impetus was the same, the recognition that the laity mattered. This helps to explain the determination of the Council of Trent to establish an imposing, educated, active and closely supervised clergy, resident in every parish.

Most striking of all, the laity were associated in the eucharist. In Protestant churches, the move to communion in both kinds, where everyone now received the wine as well as the bread, identified layman with priest. In the Church of England steps were taken to make the minister's hands visible to the congregation at the time when he consecrated the elements. Thomas Muntzer's consecration prayer was said by the whole Anabaptist congregation as a corporate priestly body. The Council of Trent issued directives to secure during mass a greater participation of the laity 'about the altar of the Lord'.

In the realm of Christian thinking, the greatest recovery for the laity was the Protestant recognition that the church is the whole people of God, a realization embodied in the doctrine of the priesthood of all believers. To quote Luther: 'The Creed indicates what the Church is clearly, namely, A Communion of Saints, that is a group or assembly of such people as are Christians and holy.' Individuals who by faith are 'in Christ' become one with each other and there are, in consequence, no distinctions in kind among believers.

> There is neither priest nor layman, canon or vicar, rich or poor, Benedictine, Carthusian, Friar Minor or Augustinian, for it is not a question of this or that status, degree or order.

Before God, said Luther – and Calvin and all the other reformers agreed – all Christians are equal. They belong to a priesthood entered by baptism and faith, in which each individual offers, as a priest, the daily sacrifice of himself, in praise and obedience to God and in bearing the cross.[5]

Only in the more extreme sects was the priesthood of all believers taken to mean that there was no longer a need for clergy. Mainstream Protestantism retains a recognized ministry, but the nature of that ministry is now changed. It is no longer a matter of a separation in kind, but of a difference in office and vocation. To quote Luther again:

> Let everyone therefore who knows himself to be a Christian be assured of this, and apply it to himself, that we are all priests

and there is no difference between us: that is to say we have the same power in respect to the Word and Sacraments. However, no one may make use of this power except by consent of the community or the call of the superior. For what is the common property of all, no individual may arrogate to himself, unless he is called.[6]

Even sects which ostensibly rejected separate clergy, notably the Quakers, are not far removed from this position, for they do not so much reject clergy as deny the concept of laity. For them the whole Christian community comes under the highest standards and performs the highest functions.

The ebbing of the tide

By the early seventeenth century, therefore, the position of the layman was in the practice of all churches, significantly different from that of his ancestor a century before, and in Protestant churches there had been a fundamental change in doctrine. The impetus did not last. A general relaxation of religious temper later in the century, the development of new clerical establishments in the Protestant denominations, the concentration of attention and effort upon the theological skirmishes of the rival creeds, the importance in time of persecution of priest and pastor, as both leader and target, all these caused the tide against clerisy to turn. The attempts to provide a more competent and learned clergy – excessively erudite in certain circles – opened once again the educational gap between cleric and layman. Instead of the one-time primacy of the clergyman as the literate man of the community, there grew up his primacy as the academically-trained man of the community. The fixation of society with order and hierarchy was, certainly in Europe, a barrier to the doctrine of the priesthood of all believers ever becoming much more than a theological abstraction. In England a revival of the value of tithes made the Anglican ministry an attractive career for gentlemen and produced the phenomenon of the 'squarson'.

But the tide did not ebb completely. There was no return to a distinction in kind between the Protestant clergy and laity. And there was no possibility of restoring entirely the foundations of lay subservience. A vigorous adherence to the priesthood of all believers was destructive of a church struggling to teach obedience, and one by one its pillars crumbled. Men began to assert that the Spirit of God could speak in the individual and even more in the group. The doctrine of the 'inner light' was not the sole preserve of the Quakers. In England, once the repressive state censorship was removed in 1640, men appeared saying what they believed, not repeating what they had been taught. Traditionalists, such as the puritan Ephraim Pagitt, cried out in vain at this dangerous impertinence. Who were these men?

> Since the suspension of our Church-government every one that listeth turneth Preacher...takes upon them to expound the holy Scriptures, intrude into our Pulpits and vent strange doctrines tending to faction, sedition and blasphemy....Whence come they now, from the schools of the Prophets? No, many of them from mechanic trades, as one from a stable from currying his horses: another from his stall from cobbling his shoes: and these sit down in Moses' chair to mend all as Ambassadors of Jesus Christ, as Heralds of the Most High God: these take upon them to reveal the secrets of almighty God, to open and shut heaven, to save men's souls.[7]

It was in vain. The recognition that the laity, just as much as the clergy, are the people of God was a powerful solvent of the habit of dependence, in ideas and in politics. The Bible is the greatest revolutionary manifesto ever written.

One of Karl Marx's most quoted remarks is 'religion...is the opium of the people', and the fact that the saying has endured indicates that there is truth in it. But we cannot reduce religion to an opiate for the under-privileged and nothing more. Equally, we cannot attribute to religion a necessarily sedative effect. In the Reformation, we can see ordinary people asserting, through religion, their claim to matter. And despite the later reaction, this claim was not lost. The door had been opened, irreversibly, to individual conscience and individual interpretation. Perhaps this led to secularism; it certainly led to the fissive tendency in nonconformity. But it freed the minds of men. The flood of consequent ideas first attracts attention in the English Civil War, but it flows to this day. Human dignity owes at least something to the Reformation. Christianity has not always been synonymous with the establishment at prayer.

Notes and references
1 Deuteronomy 22:10.
2 *The Layman in Christian History*, ed. S.Neill and H.R.Weber, SCM, 1963, p. 113.

3 *English Historical Documents 1485–1558*, ed. C.H.Williams, Eyre and Spottiswoode, 1967, p. 684.

4 J.E.Neale, *Elizabeth and Her Parliaments, 1559–1581*, Jonathan Cape, 1953, p. 205.

5 E.G.Rupp, *The Righteousness of God*, Hodder and Stoughton, 1953, p. 313; Neill and Weber, *Layman in Christian History*, p. 138.

6 Rupp, *Righteousness of God*, p. 316.

7 Ephraim Pagitt, *Heresiography*, 1645, sig. B 3v, C4.

Conclusion

Earthenware pots

Writing of the final destruction of paganism in the Roman Empire, Edward Gibbon made much of the absorption by Christianity of elements from paganism. 'The religion of Constantine achieved, in less than a century, the final conquest of the Roman Empire: but the victors themselves were insensibly subdued by the arts of their vanquished rivals.'[1]

This comment expresses a continuing truth about Christianity – that it is a vulnerable faith. To examine its record is to find love, joy and sanctity and, equally, unworthiness, periodic decadence, outbursts of hypocrisy and some evident evil: Bernardino of Siena against the anti-pope John XXIII, Little Bilney against Philip of Hesse. And more than these contrasts, it is to find that the highest expressions of Christianity are flawed by humanity – a longing for deeper spirituality ending up as religious war, a vision of the people of God debased into clerical privilege, men of God justifying violence in the service of the 'man of sorrows'. When the historian meets Christianity, the first thing he notices is its frailty.

Yet he would be wrong to conclude that when the chips are down it is the material which always counts with a man, not the spiritual. A liability to distortion is part of Christianity, a consequence of its nature. An appeal to individual men to take up day by day and voluntarily, the cross of selflessness will never achieve a total response in anyone, and no response made today can be counted on for tomorrow. The saint knows how unsanctified he can really be, and as John Bunyan wrote, 'I saw that there was a way to Hell, even from the Gates of Heaven'.[2]

The story of the Christian religion and its influence could only have been a story of continuous advance if the religion had ceased to be Christian, if it had substituted for the allegiance which changes the hearts of men a formality of credal rote and liturgical mechanics. Indeed, some of Christianity's greatest disasters have come precisely when the church has been tempted to follow this road. Christianity offers to revolutionize men and society, but it can do so only to the extent to which men and society are willing to be freed from the existence which is partly their inheritance and partly their own creation. The possibility of religious war was inherent in the Reformation as the possibility of exploitation was inherent in the very notion of a church. To use the striking metaphor of Paul, God's message is in the earthenware pot of our humanity.

If the first conclusion from a scrutiny of history and Christianity in the early modern period of Western Europe is that we must accept imperfection as a necessary risk in Christianity, the second must be that the faith is frustrated less by persecution or neglect than by compromise. We have seen the church gulped by the state, and worse than this, for in many cases its spiritual functions and authority were prostituted to political ends. There can have been few religious obscenities to equal the Test Act which made the taking of communion in an Anglican church a prerequisite for public office. Everywhere pressure can be seen upon the Christian community to conform to the world around, everywhere the dilemma which resulted from the inability of Christians singly and collectively to recognize that what was good for their earthly society and its values was not necessarily synonymous with the good of the Kingdom of God. In all too few instances have we heard the prophetic voice. The environment effectively throttled the church and prevented its operating as the spokesman of Christ. There is plenty to suggest that the pot was, indeed, made of earthenware.

But the pot is not the whole story; there is the divine power of its contents. Alongside the frailty and the conformity we have to set the reality of spiritual commitment. The sixteenth century saw the pressure for a more vital personal religion. The fact that Bible-smuggling happened to be good business and that William Tyndale was a pungent controversialist does not make discreditable the determination to put the English Bible into the hands of the common people. We may not be able to measure the increase, if any, in committed Christians in that century, but the energies of all groups in the religious conflict did lead to an increase in the depth of commitment; we need only look at what men bought to read.

The influence of Christianity can also be seen in the attitude to the community. In England, the vision of a Christian commonwealth encouraged men to public and private action. In Europe as a whole, Christians of all denominations insisted that social and economic relationships should be based on morality and, contrary to popular misconstruction, stood as a barrier to the triumph of a purely business ethic. There were even men and communities who resisted the automatic acceptance of war and violence, people who, in G.R.Elton's phrase, had the temerity to believe that Christ meant what he said about peace. In Protestant communions and even in the Tridentine Catholic Church there was a recognition of the importance of the individual church-member, not exclusively the institution.

 Religious motivation is not the whole story, but we do disservice to the truth if we leave it out in the way that seems fashionable today. Marx and Engels insisted that the economic situation is the ultimately determining element in history, but dismissed as 'meaningless, abstract, senseless' the notion that it was the only determining element. As Engels wrote:

> The economic situation is the basis, but the various elements of the superstructure: political forms of the class struggle and its results, to wit: constitutions established by the victorious class after a successful battle, etc., juridical forms, and then even the reflexes of all these actual struggles in the brains of the participants, political, juristic, philosophical theories, religious views and their further development into systems of dogmas, also exercise their influence upon the course of the historical struggles and in many cases preponderate in determining their *form*.[3]

It is not necessary to accept the original premise to see here a much needed plea for us to recognize multiple causation in history including, in its own right, religion and religious ideas.

For some there is yet another conclusion to be drawn from the study of Christianity and history in this period, the vital need for unity in religion. Certainly the challenges of the time were grasped in contradictory ways by conflicting groups. There was no sense of a united Christian community searching out a collective mind; any unanimity owed more to shared traditions than to common effort. It is also likely that the conflicts of these years helped to undermine the authority of organized religion and to reduce the role of Christianity in human affairs. An enormous energy and enthusiasm was invested in self-cancelling controversy, and it often appears that disputants were more concerned to defeat one another than to advance the cause of the Lord they each acknowledged. No doubt putting Foxe's *Book of Martyrs* in every church gave a fillip to English nationalism and helped to fix the hatred of Rome, but did it increase devotion to Christ?

Against this, however, it may be doubted whether religion would have kept its authority even if the Christian world had retained its unity; the growth of science would, by itself, have spelled the end of a monolithic religious formulation of thought. Even more important, it is arguable whether increased spiritual energy could have been contained within a united ecclesiastical organization, especially one which was also an estate in society. Increased religious zeal and coercive religious institutions may have been incompatible. The story of Christianity is a story of the constraints of the earthenware pot upon its explosive contents and of what happens when those constraints fail.

To study the relationships between Christianity and history is not to arrive at dogmatic certainty or to establish what the faithful necessarily want to hear. But it is to assert the claim that Christian belief has been important and far from the simplistic conditioning it is often thought to be. Gain against loss, the dynamic against the status quo, the earthenware pot and the spirit which it imprisons and which destroys it, this is what Christianity in history is all about.

Notes and references
1 Edward Gibbon, *The Decline and Fall of the Roman Empire*, Oxford University Press, 1904, vi.254.
2 John Bunyan, *The Pilgrim's Progress*, ed. R. Sharrock, Penguin, 1965, p. 205.
3 Friedrich Engels to J.Bloch, 21/22 September, 1890.

JOHN CALVIN
T.H.L.Parker

Even today the name of John Calvin arouses strong reactions. Was he an unbending tyrant – or a theologian of genius?

In this first full-scale life of Calvin for nearly forty years Dr Parker builds up an impressive portrait of the man whose ideas became among the most revolutionary in Europe.

T.H.L.Parker, a specialist on Calvin and Geneva, paints a vivid picture of conflict and change in the Reformation world. Making full use of recent research, he tells of the young Calvin's student days in France. But central to the story is Calvin's fierce love–hate relationship with Geneva, where he wrote and preached with boundless energy and love, in his efforts to build a godly society. Parker analyses concisely Calvin's classic presentation of the Christian faith, *The Institutes*.

Dr Parker lectures in theology at the University of Durham, and is widely known as an authority on Calvin. His previous books include *Oracles of God* (the first English study of Calvin's preaching), *Portrait of Calvin* and *Calvin's New Testament*.

'An interesting, lively, reliable and workmanlike treatment of the life of John Calvin.' *Professor James Atkinson, University of Sheffield*

WILBERFORCE
John Pollock

This major new biography of the reformer who led the campaign to abolish the slave trade is only the second to appear in the last fifty years. John Pollock presents a fully-rounded and delightful portrait of Wilberforce, claiming, against the critics, that he was 'neither politically repressive nor personally dreary.'

'One of the most moving and memorable historical biographies in our time . . . It should on no account be missed.' *Church Times*

'Mr Pollock gives an excellent account of the campaign against the slave trade and slavery . . . A very fine and informative book.' *Church of England Newspaper*

'This biography is the product of much painstaking research. John Pollock has made use of virtually all the extant manuscript collections containing Wilberforce materials . . . He gives a detailed picture of his life and character which includes some important new information.' *The Observer*

John Pollock has written a number of popular biographies, and his books have been translated into ten languages. Over 1¼ million copies are in print in English alone.

KARL MARX
David Lyon

Karl Marx claimed that the chains of the exploited were obscured by the flowers of ideology and religion. He set out both to remove the flowers and to break the chains. But was his solution really radical enough?

This book traces the development of Marx' ideas against his nineteenth-century background: his early life and writings, the 1848 revolutions, Marx' major work in economics, his views of history, class, women and property. Trade unionism and revolution are major topics.

The book is not only a biography: it is also an analysis of Marx' ideas from a Christian viewpoint. As such it shares a concern, not just for Marx in history, but for the way his ideas are working today.

Dr David Lyon is Senior Lecturer in Sociology at Ilkley College, West Yorkshire. He was Visiting Assistant Professor in the Department of Sociology and Anthropology at Wilfrid Laurier University, Ontario, in 1976–77.

PSYCHOLOGY AS RELIGION
Paul Vitz

This book is a forthright and thought-provoking
critique of modern psychology. The subject has
become not a science but a religion. And as a religion
it is a false one, based on self-ism and leading to self-
worship.

Paul Vitz, Associate Professor of Psychology at New
York University, has been forced to a radical reap-
praisal of his subject. He analyses modern approaches to psychology, examining them from scientific, philosophical, ethical, economic and religious
points of view. He challenges the cult of self-help, and
the fad of blaming psychological maladjustment on
the family. And he presents a positive, alternative way
of looking at people and their problems based on the
realistic Christian assessment of human nature he
himself has rediscovered.

'A completely justified cry of alarm. The danger in
psychology of a serious confusion between science
and philosophy, between the observation of
phenomena and their interpretation, increases with
the success of the discipline. Professor Vitz shows this
with clarity and thereby renders us a great service.'
Paul Tournier

'It says what ought to have been said long ago – brave-
ly, clearly and constructively.'
Karl Menninger

'If this is the 'Me' decade, here is its essence. Paul Vitz
holds a mirror to our times and captures its real face
behind the cosmetic image. Penetrating and absor-
bing, his book is invaluable reading.'
Os Guinness

MAHALIA
Laurraine Goreau

'Don't make me no saint, baby! Tell the real story of me,' Mahalia Jackson told her chosen biographer, Laurraine Goreau. This is the real story, accurate, carefully researched – yet breathing the true spirit of a dynamic and endearingly human woman.

At breathless pace we follow Mahalia from the poverty of New Orleans – streets vibrating to the rhythm of ragtime jazz – through troubles and triumphs to eventual wealth and worldwide acclaim. Turning her back on 'the Devil's music' – jazz and blues – Mahalia soared to fame on the holy beat of Gospel, becoming one of the all-time greats.

She was a woman of uncompromising integrity and almost childlike faith. Yet she had to fight all the way – fight for success, for the basic human rights of black Americans, and for health and happiness. She found fame, but not without failure. Generous, warm-hearted, loving to surround herself with family and friends, Mahalia walked alone.

Her story is written by a close friend, Laurraine Goreau, who is also an editor, musician and dramatist.

SUMMER IN THE CITY
Malcolm Doney

Rock is more than music. It is a way of life. It promises freedom, challenges the establishment, creates a new lifestyle.

'Rock is the story of people's lives, mine included,' writes Malcolm Doney. He tells of people and groups, the music, the stars and the fans. But the aim is not just to retell the story, but to ask questions. What are these promises of a new life and a new lifestyle? Do they have any basis, any reality? Is this really the way of freedom?

Just when the movement seemed to be played out, new-wave Rock brought it sharply to life again. So the story of Rock is not just a matter of history. As an artist and now a journalist with the Christian news magazine *Crusade*, Malcolm Doney believes it is crucial for understanding the world in which we live, for understanding what is happening to us, to know what the music, the whole Rock movement, is saying.